# SILVER SPOON

# Silver Spoon

M. A. SPENCER-NAIRN

The Pentland Press
Edinburgh – Cambridge – Durham – USA

First published in 1996 by
The Pentland Press Ltd
1 Hutton Close
South Church
Bishop Auckland
Durham

ISBN 1-85821-343-6

Typeset by Carnegie Publishing, 18 Maynard St, Preston
Printed and bound by Antony Rowe Ltd, Chippenham

# Contents

*Foreword* . . . . . . . . . . . . . . . . . . . . vii

Chapter 1   Barham . . . . . . . . . . . . . . . . . . . . . . . 1

Chapter 2   School . . . . . . . . . . . . . . . . . . . . . . . 10

Chapter 3   Early days at Leslie . . . . . . . . . . . . . . . 18

Chapter 4   Glenshirra . . . . . . . . . . . . . . . . . . . . . 23

Chapter 5   Trains and Shrewsbury . . . . . . . . . . . . . 31

Chapter 6   Back at Leslie . . . . . . . . . . . . . . . . . . . 37

Chapter 7   Cambridge . . . . . . . . . . . . . . . . . . . . . 44

Chapter 8   Kintail and Cambridge . . . . . . . . . . . . . 52

Chapter 9   Linoleum . . . . . . . . . . . . . . . . . . . . . . 64

Chapter 10  The Territorial Army . . . . . . . . . . . . . . 71

Chapter 11  Australia and New Zealand . . . . . . . . . . 79

Chapter 12  Home again. I get engaged . . . . . . . . . . . 90

Chapter 13     Marriage . . . . . . . . . . . . . . . . . . . . . . 97

Chapter 14     The start of married life . . . . . . . . . . . . . 102

Chapter 15     The start at Balgeddie . . . . . . . . . . . . . . 113

Chapter 16     The War starts . . . . . . . . . . . . . . . . . . 120

Chapter 17     Post-war readjustment . . . . . . . . . . . . . . 139

Chapter 18     That fateful year . . . . . . . . . . . . . . . . . 159

Chapter 19     Mostly travel . . . . . . . . . . . . . . . . . . . 168

Chapter 20     West Hall . . . . . . . . . . . . . . . . . . . . . 176

Chapter 21     Retiral . . . . . . . . . . . . . . . . . . . . . . . 182

Chapter 22     My faith and where it led me . . . . . . . . . 203

Appendix     Nairns of Kirkcaldy . . . . . . . . . . . . . . . 208

# Foreword

This little book, for what it is worth, started as a therapy and would never have been completed without the encouragement of my wife, family and many friends. It certainly would not have been written without the help of many members of the Fife Society for the Blind. They first taught me to touch type on an electric typewriter and then promoted me to this wonderful computer which is fitted with a miraculous voice box. A special word of thanks must also go to David Weir who not only taught me all I know of the secrets of this machine, but rescued me when I strayed into the wilderness and set me back on my little lane along the fringe. I shall never forget Jayne Neilson who not only corrected many of the chapters as they appeared but read all the galley proofs to me. Finally, there is Philip Mackie who greatly encouraged me and introduced me to publishers.

My memory is suspect, so there may be errors of detail, such as dates or names. I take full responsibility for such and make my apologies now.

# CHAPTER I

# Barham

My parents were married on 13 February 1906 and took up residence at Barham, Springfield, Fife. I shall always remember that address as nine years later it was the one I had to write to from Cargilfield in going to prep. school. Barham was situated about five hundred yards west of the Bow of Fife, on the Cupar–Auchtermuchty road. My elder brother Douglas was born there on 24 December the same year. I think it must have been early in 1908 that my parents decided to enlarge Barham and they took a lease of Eden Park House, Cupar, for the period of the alterations. It was there on 13 January 1909 that I entered this world. I was much too young to remember when the work was completed and we moved back to Barham, but the records show it was December of that year. Some time during 1910 I had diphtheria and scarlet fever. My younger brother Frank was born in November 1910.

I think the postal address of Barham is now Cupar. In those days there were no vans for the delivery of mail; it was delivered to Springfield by train. From there our postman walked by way of Rankeilour East Lodge, the farm, and then to the Mansion House. From there he continued down the west drive and then turned right through a small path through the wood, emerging at the postman's steps opposite the entrance to Pitlair. These stone steps were built into the wall and are still there. Postie then called at Pitlair, Daft Mill and so round to Barham. From Barham he made his deliveries in the Bow before picking up the mail from the little post office. So, having almost emptied his bag, he now had it partially filled again. A call at Over Rankeilour farm completed his round and he returned to Springfield.

Unlike many children I cannot remember any of the house staff, although there were nanny, nurse-maid, cook, table-maid and probably a house-maid as well. One person whom I do remember was my mother's lady's maid, Andy, who came from a farm between Nairn and Elgin. She eventually married Tom Methven of Over Rankeilour Farm.

The outside staff I remember better. The head gardener was an elderly man and was rather bent. He lived at the front lodge. The under-gardener was called Davidson and he lived at the Bow. I expect I remember him because he had two children, Charlie and Betty. They were slightly older than us but were very good at playing with us. Mrs Davidson was also very good to us. Father's groom chauffeur was David Strachan, but I can remember little of him. When father was called up in 1914 he went with him as groom, and I don't think he returned after the war. David was replaced by Mathers, a typical bow-legged groom. I suspect he was unfit for military service. Poor Mathers, he had a wife but he always looked under-fed and henpecked. His wife proved to be mentally unstable and finally tried to drown herself in the burn. It was sad for Mathers but a great excitement for us when she was taken away to the asylum.

Father's hunter, which went as his charger, was replaced by a pony called Sir Renalds. We used to ride this pony accompanied by Mathers on a bicycle. He also went in a governess cart in which Mathers drove my mother.

Most of my memories must apply to the war years as I was only five and a half when the war started. There were three other families in the Bow who must be mentioned. There was Joanne Baldie who pumped the organ in church on Sunday; then there was Miss Page who kept the small shop and post office. Finally there was the Rev. Beattie and his wife and daughter. He was a most delightful man with a beard, and to us seemed to be very old, but was probably only in his late sixties. Mrs Beattie and her daughter were an odd couple. If you met them out walking they would never speak to you but turned and looked over the wall until you had passed. If we were ever sent with a message or something for Mr Beattie we never went to the door of the manse but knocked on the window of Mr Beattie's study. I don't know what sort of a welcome other parishoners received at the manse door.

While on this subject, there were two elders whom I shall always remember as they were both head gardeners. John Reid, who was head gardener at Rankeilour, always struck me as a rather austere man. John Brown, on the other hand, who was head gardener at Fernie Castle, was full of fun. They both walked to church each Sunday dressed in their best suits and bowler hats. Before going to church we had to be very sure that Flossie, father's springer spaniel, was firmly shut up as otherwise she would, if the door was open, join us in the gallery or if the church door was shut would bark to be let in.

There was one thing which I never enjoyed in those early years, but which only occurred in the winter. This was being dressed up in a sailor suit and sent down to the drawing-room at five o'clock. We were then allowed to play with toys for fifty minutes before the toys had to be tidied up before nanny collected us for bath and bed at six o'clock.

Twice a week Mr Opdale, the baker from Ladybank, would arrive seated high up on his horse-drawn articulated baker's van. The van was drawn by a single horse and was still fitted with iron-clad wheels. When the double doors at the back were opened there was a delightful smell of fresh bread. Those lovely tall double Scottish loaves formed the bulk of what was on offer but there were other loaves, cookies and cakes. Under the main chamber there were two deep drawers, one filled with girdle scones and the other with drop scones and other goodies.

Another fairly regular visitor was Dr Douglas who came by car. He was a little man with very prominent veins on his face and enormous ears. He was a great friend to all the family and especially to my mother. He brought all but one of us into the world. I must not forget the car, which was reputed to be one of the first in Cupar. It had a little square bonnet, with of course a bright brass radiator cap. In front of that there were two large lamps which I think must have been paraffin. There was a little low windscreen and a single bench seat. The steering column went vertically down through the floor and of course the wheel was parallel to the ground. Behind the seat there was a small flat area on which rested the hood. When pulled up over the seat this was secured by a strap on either side secured to a D on the front mudguard. This magnificent machine was driven by his ex-coachman, dressed in breeches, black boots and leggings, a high buttoned tunic and a cap. At least, that is as how I remember it.

On 12 July 1913 Matilda my eldest sister was born. The extraordinary thing is that I can remember nothing of the event, except that Frank joined me in the north room and Douglas moved to father's dressing-room.

Health-wise we were a very normal family. We were fed on Robaline, a sticky brown malt mixture which we enjoyed. Every so often we were given a dose of Gregory's powder. This was a pink powder which came in measured doses, very neatly folded in paper. The powder was sprinkled onto a little water in a spoon which was then thrust into your mouth. It was claggy stuff which you could not get rid of. I suffered from what were called growing pains in my legs, and was treated by being submerged in a very hot bath into which there had been added some special salts. After cooking for a time I was taken out, wrapped in a towel and a blanket and put into bed wet. The cure worked.

Early in 1915 some of us, I don't remember how many, had our tonsils removed on the nursery table. I remember little about it except for the sore throat.

From time to time Mother would take some of us on her shopping visits to Cupar. Her regular ports of call were: Anderson the

Frank, Douglas, Matilda, Alastair.

butcher, Campbell's or Kerricker the fishmongers; Reid's the
grocer; Whitelaw, the chemist, Miss Elders the baker; and Miss
Hutton at the china shop.

What characters these were. I can still see Miss Hutton standing
amongst all the glass and china in her long black skirt and black
pork pie straw hat. We used to go and buy vases for Mother's
birthday, but I am sure the real cost was charged to Mother's
account. Then there was Mr Whitelaw, looking over his thin wire
glasses and surrounded by all his bottles. Walton's was the garage
where we got cans of petrol. Another person I can remember is old
Mr Osborne with his head of white hair. His daughter Polly became
a firm friend of my mother.

Barham being quite close to Rankeilour, we either walked over
or were driven over to see my grandparents. My grandfather, the

first Sir Michael Barker Nairn, was a short, thick man with a large
white beard. We wondered why he did not catch his beard on fire
with his cigarettes which he would leave in his mouth with a long
curving ash on the end. My grandmother was a very neat little
woman with dark hair parted in the middle with very few traces of
grey. We all loved her, but our grandfather was a little off-putting.
Living at home at that time before the war were Aunt Fanny, Aunt
Edith, and Aunt Dorothy.

My grandfather had a large family, eleven in all. They were: Katie
who married William Black, who worked in the company in Kirkcaldy; then Fanny who never married; followed by Effie who married Harry Nicholson, a doctor in Edinburgh. Then came Edith
who married Jim Holroyd; and I think Michael (the next Sir Michael) who married Mildred Neish. Next came Tibby who married
John Thomson-Walker who later became a famous London surgeon. After that came Mary who married Willie Balfour and they
lived in Fernie Castle. Robert, my father, was next; then Dorothy
who married an Australian, Bruce Thomas; and finally Douglas who
died aged about fourteen, and Lucy who died very young. We will
meet several of these again as my story unfolds.

My grandfather had two cars, both Argyles. The old one was
chain driven and made the most awful noise. The chauffeur was
called Milne.

My grandmother, whose maiden name had been Spencer, had two
brothers: Alfred, who was older than her and Henry who was
considerably younger. Alfred, who was of very low IQ, often came
to stay at Rankeilour. He was a small thin man and he always wore
a velvet skull cap when in the house. I don't think he ever had a
job of any kind. His occupation was reading *The Times*, which he
did with the aid of a magnifying glass. He would come out with
some surprising questions, sometimes about things which he had
read about in the paper. Normally he lived in digs in Aberdour. His
life revolved round his newspaper and his watch. He would walk
to the post office each day to check that it was correct. There was

a famous occasion when he dressed himself up in his frock coat and with top hat, umbrella and gloves, set off for Edinburgh. He walked to the station, got the train times to and from Edinburgh, and off he went. Nobody knows what he did in Edinburgh but he knew that his return train was due to leave at 4.15 so, arriving at Waverley in good time, he found a train leaving at 4.15. He boarded it and off it went. It should have arrived at Aberdour at 4.35, but his train did not stop. When, some time later, it did stop he got out and walked to the barrier to give up his ticket where he was told that he was not at Aberdour but at Galashiels. The station master was summoned and took compassion on him. He put my uncle on the next train back to Edinburgh, and telephoned Waverley and arranged for him to be met and put on a train home.

Of our Nairn aunts Aunt Dorothy was our favourite, probably because she was the youngest, but in any case she was always full of fun. It took me a long time before I discovered that Father Christmas was Aunt Dorothy. She gave me a Bible when I went to boarding school and I have it to this day.

My mother was also one of a large family: five boys and four girls. The younger two of her three sisters, Aunts Con and Helen, often came to stay as did her younger brother Uncle Bull (Alack). It was through him that I got my nickname Kay. He used to refer to me as the real McKay but Douglas could not say McKay so it got shortened to Kay, the name which is used by my brother and sisters to this day.

During those early years we had little contact with other children, especially during the war years, owing to petrol shortage. We occasionally saw Peter and Betty Haig from Ramornie, Hugh and Elizabeth Sharp from Hill of Tarvit, the Lumsdens from Tarvit and the Kerrs from Over Rankeilour. The family we saw most of was the Lindsays. Major Lindsay had been appointed adjutant to the Fife and Forfar Yeomanry. They lived at first at Lathrisk but moved to Craigfoodie, Dairsie, which became their permanent home. At that time there were three boys of similar ages to Douglas, myself

and Frank. Their names were Pom, Michael and Bill. We will meet
them again. Our Nairn cousins lived in Dysart which was a long
way away so we seldom saw them.

My mother started our education, She taught us the ABC, as we
called it, and to count, but, what is far more important, she taught
us about Jesus and to pray. As soon as we could talk she would
come to say good night to us and we would say our little prayer:
'God bless Daddy and Mummy and make me a good boy, Amen.'
Each day after lunch we were made to lie on our backs on the
smoking room floor and she would read to us. On Sunday it was
Bible stories. As we grew older we came under Miss Christie, our
governess who came daily from Cupar. She was very nice but I
think found three small boys rather too much. However she kept
us going until we went to our prep. school.

In the spring of 1915 the Fife and Forfar were stationed at Fakenham in Norfolk. Suddenly, in June, my mother announced that
she was going to take us down to join father. We were to go by
night sleeper to London, and then on to Surrey to spend a day or
two with her mother and sisters. The day came, we were put to bed
as usual and then at the appropriate time were roused: stockings on,
shoes on, dressing gowns on and finally great coats. We left Barham
with about half an hour to spare for punctures. It was lucky we did
as, sure enough, we did have a puncture. There was considerable
panic but Mathers had the wheel changed in good time and we still
had to wait at the station. I shared a bunk with I think Douglas.
After breakfast at King's Cross we taxied to Victoria and so down
to Cobham. The Grange was a fairly large house and it needed to
be because there were Granny, Aunts Ethel, Con and Helen, and
our party. I can remember little of the place except that the gardener
had a large wire cage outside his house which was connected to a
window in his house by a wire tunnel. In this cage there were a
number of red squirrels which came and went freely into the house
by the tunnel.

From Cobham we travelled by train to Fakenham. At first we

stayed in the Rectory at Scunthorpe and later moved to the Rectory at Fakenham. Mrs Lindsay (Elsie) had brought her three boys down and I think lived next door to us. Anyway we used to play together in the hay.

The thing I remember best was catching whooping cough. I was terrified when the whoops came as I could not get my breath. We were looked after by the Regimental doctor. Tukie used to arrive by horse-drawn ambulance with a huge red cross on the side. Then, in September, the Regiment went off to Galipoli and we returned home. Father along with many others got dysentery and was evacuated to Cairo and then home. I think he was posted to a staff job in Glasgow. He must have arrived home in the summer of 1916.

It was probably in June of that year before Father's return that we travelled to Nairn for our summer holiday. We went of course by train and had a special sort of drawing-room on it. Even in the war the train was met by a piper at Aviemore station. I think the train split there, the front half going on to Inverness and the back to the coast. We stayed in a boarding house. We boys visited the slaughter house, got chased by a farmer for sitting on his gate, and had similar adventures. One day Andy took us to her home where they were making hay. I remember being given lemonade from one of those bottles with a glass ball as a stopper.

The big exploit was a day trip to Cawdor Castle. We went with a picnic lunch in a horse drawn barouche pulled by a grey horse.

My second sister Claire was born on 30 April 1917. As with Matilda, I remember nothing of the event.

Douglas went to Cargilfield in September 1915 and I followed in January 1918.

# CHAPTER 2

# School

Leaving home for boarding school was a great change, although it was made much easier for me having an older brother to go with. Some time before the fateful day I had been taken to Edinburgh to be kitted out at Gulland and Kennedy in George Street. When the day came our little hand bags were packed and we were ready. These bags were made of leather and opened along the top, just like the traditional doctor's bag did. I don't remember how our school trunks got to the station although they were sent 'luggage to be delivered', but I can remember horse drawn lorries arriving at school loaded with school trunks. We were put on the train at Ladybank and on arrival at Waverley found other Cargilfield boys. Several of us piled into a horse drawn cab and set off for Cargilfield. The journey was nearly four miles and took almost an hour. There were few if any taxis owing to the shortage of fuel. The Edinburgh single decker buses were fuelled by coal gas, each bus having a gas bag the full length of its roof which used to flap in the wind as it became empty.

I don't remember many of the staff, but they were nearly all elderly, all young people having left for war work. The headmaster was Mr Thomas. Three other masters and the matron had been in post when my father had been there. These included Mr Benbow and two other elderly ones and Mr Cramner who had been wounded in the war and was now unfit for military service. The matron's name I have forgotten but she was known to all boys as Gutsie.

On arrival I was a very timid and backward little boy and it was quickly decided that I required extra tuition in reading. This I did with Mrs Cramner. Every week there was a period called reports when we all assembled in one large classroom. There the weekly reports were read out. If your report was too bad you were sent to the headmaster. You stood in a queue outside his study door and listened intently to hear how many your predecessor got. When your turn came you entered, received a very short telling off, and were then bent over and received your beating. The instrument used was rather like a squash racket with a solid end. It made a lot of noise and stung a bit but did not cause any bruising.

The school was still lit only by carbide gas. The gas was made by Johnnie who also came round at lighting up time and lit all the lamps. Johnnie looked after the swimming bath in the summer term and I have no doubt that he did many other jobs as well.

At one time I was in a dormitory which looked out over the back yard. There there were large wooden barrels into which was put the garbage. We used to pop out through the window and with a piece of stick would prop open the wooden lid, then when the starlings flew in we would pull out the stick with a piece of string and thereby trap them. Most of them got away but we did catch a few which we put in a box under our beds. I cannot remember what happened to them finally.

At the entrance which we boys used there was a sort of lean-to porch. Every summer a swallow nested under that roof and the nest was never touched.

I remember going a school run where we went by Davidson's Mains, down the Queensferry Road and back past the ruins of old Barnton House. On Sunday, dressed in our kilts and Eton collars, we walked to Cramond Church.

In November 1918 we all walked down to Cramond to watch the German fleet brought in. The British ships were on the outside and the Germans in the middle. They stretched right out of sight. At night the German ships were all lit up by search-lights from the British ships.

In the summer of 1919 I got terrible ear-ache, and a specialist was summoned from Edinburgh. As the result of his visit I was carted off to a nursing home in Drumsheugh Gardens where I underwent a mastoid operation. I came to to find my head swathed in bandages and I kept them on for nearly four months. While in the home they kept me occupied rolling bandages which had to be reused, as owing to the war medical requirements were in very short supply. The washed but loose bandages were brought into my room in a big basket and I was taught to roll them on one of those tables which straddled the bed.

On release from hospital my parents engaged an elderly trained nurse to look after me. Mrs Grier used to dress my wound daily which was very painful; she also injected me at regular intervals which was almost equally painful.

Two more important events occurred in 1919. The first was our first visit to Glenshirra Lodge. Glenshirra, with about 22,000 acres, was situated at the head of the River Spey. It belonged to Sir John Ramsden of Ardverickie. There was good grouse shooting and stalking, but more about this later. I did not return to school in September as my wound was not healed but I returned to Barham and joined the schoolroom.

Early in November I was taken by my parents to view Leslie House. This was the first I knew of my parents' intention to leave Barham, and it came as a great surprise. Leslie House seemed huge compared to Barham, and the visit was most exciting. We were met and shown round by Mr and Mrs Crundle. We were taken through a large hall with four large pillars, and up the broad stone stair. The walls of the stairway were hung with enormous tapestries, and I shall always remember the one on the second flight as it depicted Saul falling on his sword: a very gruesome picture. At the top of the first flight there was a curtain across the passage. We passed through the curtains and there on the wall hung an elephant's tail.

The house was full of bits and heads of African animals. Everywhere there hung the smell of scent and I gathered that Mrs Crundle made her own. We were shown over the whole house and I was thrilled, especially as I was the only member of the family to see it. I don't know when Father announced that we would be moving to Leslie, but the move took place in December 1919.

Mr Crundle was a financial man who had bought the whole of the Leslie estate from the Earl of Rothes. It had been a large estate and stretched nearly from Thornton to the top of the Lomonds. Mr Crundle sold off all the farms to the tenants and was left with the house, gardens, stables, and the policies which included two large fields, two small parks, and considerable woodlands.

Shortly after that visit I returned to Cargilfield.

The bathing arrangements at Cargilfield were quite unique. There were two steps down into a room about 15 ft by 15 ft; the whole floor was lead covered, continuing about a foot up the walls. There was a hot and cold tap at each side and all were fitted with a short length of hose, and there was a drain in the middle. There were about six round metal baths, about three feet in diameter and about nine inches deep. We filled our baths with the hoses and when finished emptied them on the floor. It did not matter how much water you threw about, a wonderful system for small boys.

I remember little of the remainder of my time at Cargilfield except that I had measles in 1920. That was the year in which Douglas had to sit his Common Entrance for Rugby. I think he must have failed as he left and a tutor, Mr Vernon, came. Mr Vernon was a very nice man who came from Shropshire, and I think he must have had a hand in all three of us going to Shrewsbury School.

What prompted my parents to take Frank and me away from Cargilfield I do not know, but we were sent to Cottesmore School in January 1921. The choice of Cottesmore, I am sure, was influenced by the fact that the Lindsay boys were there.

This move meant long train journeys as Cottesmore's address

was Upper Drive, Hove, Sussex. What a contrast there was between these two schools! Cargilfield was larger, old fashioned and spartan, where survival of the fittest was the order of the day in all departments. Cottesmore was smaller, more modern and had very much the atmosphere of a large family. I remember nothing of our arrival, but I remember lots about the school.

I think the school was the brain child of its headmaster, Geoffrey Davidson-Brown, and it had been purpose-built some time before the war. It occupied a beautiful south-facing site overlooking the playing field. There was a large central hall with a pitched roof running east–west, and on each end there were two classrooms. On the south side was the central front door, either side of which there was a master's study. On the north side there was a long passage with central door to the hall and across the passage the stair up to the dormitories. At the west end of the passage were the lavatories, showers and changing rooms, and at the other end the dining-rooms and kitchen.

The headmaster was known to all as the Baron, and the life of the school circulated round him. He was a short fat man with a bald head who smoked numerous cigarettes, always in a cigarette holder. A word or two about the routine will illustrate what I mean.

In the hall there was a large, high-backed old wooden chair at the east end. On the left of that chair was the door to the Baron's study which was never closed. There were enough flat topped desks for all boys to sit, facing the Baron of course. There was also a ping-pong table.

After breakfast each morning we all assembled in this hall and the Baron held court. Then a group would leave for the lavatory. As one boy returned another would go; the returning boy would go to the Baron's table and if successful tick off against his name (if a failure I think you left a blank). There were various other occasions when we assembled in the hall and the Baron was always either in his chair or in his study. The Baron used to have his supper on a tray in his study just about the time we went up to bed. Every so often he would ask two or three boys in; we sat and chatted and after his supper was finished we would play cards. In the summer he would take us for a run in his old open tourer car, usually along the front at Brighton.

Another ploy of the Baron's was to take two or three boys away with him in the summer holidays. At one time he owned a holiday home in the west of Ireland, but I think that was burnt down by the Black and Tans or some other Irish group. Frank and I were probably two of the luckiest as in 1923 he invited us to go to Cowes Regatta with him. Father's permission was requested and granted along with the necessary finance. On our arrival at Cowes we found ourselves housed in, believe it or not, the London Yacht Club. We shared an attic room and had breakfast and lunch in the club dining-room, but were given supper by the steward and sent to bed.

All the old gentlemen were most kind to us. On one occasion a Mr Lavine asked us to crew with him in a 10-metre class race. As we had no knowledge of sailing it was a very bold move and he obviously was not worried about winning. He said that as he weighed 20 stone he required some lighter crew members. I don't remember how the race went except that it was great fun.

The highlight of the visit was the last day. We were invited by Sir Charles Allum to join him on the *White Heather* for the day's racing. The *White Heather* was a J-class yacht, the largest class, and we were to be racing against *Britannia* with the King on board and other famous yachts such as *Shamrock*. On arrival on board we were put in charge of the professional skipper who came from the west of Scotland. It was a beautiful day but without a breath of wind. When the starting gun went the yachts were all at anchor in a line, and no one was prepared to lift his anchor for fear of drifting backwards with the tide. Eventually a little wind came and there was a scramble to get away first. We managed to make it and once out of the shelter of Cowes Bay there was plenty of wind. The yacht heeled over to a tremendous angle with the water well over the deck. We kept very still and only moved when the skipper told us to. Lunch was served in the cabin which had a balanced table which kept level regardless of the angle of the yacht. I don't recall the result of the race but if we had won I think I would have remembered.

We had been told to get ashore as soon as possible as we had to catch a ferry for Southampton to meet our father in London and return to Scotland that night. Owing to the delay at the start of the race, however, we were much later back than anticipated and we missed the ferry. Once again fortune came to our aid. We had met in the club a Mr Roe who built speed boats. He found us wondering what to do and immediately offered to run us over in one of his boats. This was another thrill and we watched our watches as we sped across, but alas, just as we were slowing down, we saw the train moving out of the station. We thanked Mr Roe profusely and went in search of a telephone to ring Father to find out what to do next. We found him, as expected, at the Bath Club. We poured out our long story and then waited for instructions.

As always, Father had the situation completely under control. We were instructed to take the next train and on arrival to report to Mr Nash, the head porter at Brown's Hotel. We had no idea what to expect on arrival at Brown's Hotel, but it was certainly not what we did find. We were fed and shown to a double room with two beds, told to go to bed and be down for breakfast at eight o'clock as we would be picked up at a quarter to nine. We did as we were told and at 8.30 were waiting in the hall to see who would pick us up and what he would do with us. We expected to be taken to King's Cross and put on a train. But why pick us up? Why were we not just put in a taxi and told to get on with it?

At 8.45 a young man appeared, and after a word at the desk collected us but without our baggage. As we walked to his car he told us that he was taking us to Wembley. The big Commonwealth Exhibition was on and all Commonwealth countries had buildings. Michael Nairn and Co. had a big stand in the British Pavilion. On arrival we reported to John Wallace, head of the company's London sales, who was in charge of our stand.

Mr Wallace put us in charge of a young salesman who was instructed to show us round the various pavilions and have us back at one o'clock. We had a most interesting morning, rushing from pavilion to pavilion so as not to miss anything. John Wallace took us to lunch and then left us at the amusement park with strict instructions to be back at the company's stand at 4.30. The amusement park was huge. There were giant racers, mystery tunnels, pretty girls in bed who could be tipped out if you could hit a target with a tennis ball, rifle ranges and thousands of other stands. 4.30 approached all too soon.

John Wallace was a most amusing man with huge black eyebrows. He became MP for Dunfermline and was knighted for his public service. He was the father of Ian Wallace, the singer.

After a long wait at Brown's, during which we had supper, we were put into a taxi and started our journey back to Kirkcaldy. What a wonderful holiday!

That year I took my Common Entrance and by some miracle must have passed as I left Cottesmore and went to Shrewsbury in January 1923.

# CHAPTER 3

# Early days at Leslie

I think a little hindsight will help to clarify the degree of affluence in which we grew up. In 1916 my grandfather, who had been a very successful businessman, died. He had only two sons, the next Sir Michael and my father. Uncle Mike inherited Dysart and Pitcarmick and my father inherited Rankeilour, and they both inherited large blocks of shares in the family company.

This occurrence and the ending of the First World War in 1918 both had a great influence on our futures.

The Leslie House to which we returned from schooling in December 1919 was a large house, but not nearly so big as it had once been. The original house had been destroyed by fire in the seventeen hundreds. The house was built across a ridge running between the Lothrie Burn on the north and the River Leven on the south. It was rectangular, three stories high, with attics above with dormer windows behind a balustrade on the west side. The front door was in the centre of the west elevation and led direct into the large entrance hall. On the opposite side of the hall there was a door leading into the Italian garden. Above the hall there was a billiard room on the west side and a lounge on the east side. On the second floor there was a ball-room stretching the full width of the house. Through an archway on the right of the hall was the front stair and through a door to the left was the back stair. Both staircases were stone built and of similar width, the only difference being that one was carpeted and the other not. To the right or south end were all the public rooms and bedrooms and to the left or north were all

Leslie House.

the kitchens, nurseries and domestic quarters. At the north end there was a stone stair leading down to a back door.

Outside the front door there was a large gravel area almost the full width of the house with, to the north, steps leading down to a path to the walled garden and the back road to the laundry and stables. The south steps led down to the terraced garden. The drive ran straight away from the house with wide lawns on either side for three to four hundred yards. At the end of the straight there was a sharp turn to the right to the Duke's Lodge and a slight curve to the right took you to the Duchess Lodge. Almost directly opposite the Duchess Lodge was the village green, behind which stood Christ's Kirk on the Green and the Manse. The original house had a north wing and a south wing enclosing a courtyard which was now the Italian garden. Stretching away from the Italian garden almost as far as the eye could see was a disused drive. There must have been four or five hundred acres of park and woodland.

Leading from the Duke's Lodge there was a back drive which passed between the Lothrie Burn and the house. From this there was access to the house through the back door. Some forty yards further on, on the right-hand side, was the laundry. This was quite a large stone-built building with a wash-room and a finishing room fitted with a stove for heating the flat irons and, of course, a mangle. The drying green was miles away and I gathered that the wet linen used to be carted there and back by a pony and cart. This road continued and eventually landed up at the home farm.

Opposite the laundry there was a lovely stone bridge crossing the Lothrie, over which a road continued up the steep bank to the stables and garage. On the left of this road was the walled garden. In the stable area there was accommodation for seven or eight horses and five cars, with a harness room, boiler house, etc. There was a groom's house with bothie above, a single cottage and a keeper's house and kennels. My father built a new house for the head chauffeur, who was also in charge of the stables. Slightly to the west was the back gate and lodge and then left again the gardener house and bothie. Can you imagine a better opportunity for exploration for three small boys aged twelve, ten, and eight? We never needed to have a dull moment for in wet weather we were allotted a large room in the south-west corner on the third floor as a playroom.

Then there was Leslie town to explore. It was quite a sizeable country town and stretched west for about two miles. The largest employer was Smith Anderson's paper mill.

I could go on for hours describing our many adventures in these new surroundings but there is one institution I must mention. Douglas's birthday was on 24 December and a children's party was arranged on that date for the next seventeen or eighteen years. Oh, how I hated those occasions! All the boys would stand at one side of the room and all the girls at the other, then some parent would come and seize you by the hand, drag you across the room, pick up a girl and thrust you into an eightsome reel or some other dance.

I never knew what to do and had no ambition to learn. There was one ghastly occasion when it was to be a fancy dress party. Mother had bought the outfits and I was to be dressed as a jester.

That afternoon I was playing with some other boys with a billy goat up at the stables. The goat rushed up the outside stair to the bothie and onto the roof. I followed and slipped and fell to the ground. I was unhurt except for a cricked neck. I arrived home with my head on one side and full of hope of escaping the party, but alas, it was not to be. All the sympathy I got was: your clothes stink of that goat, go and get dressed. Never have I spent a more miserable evening. As the family grew so the time and nature of the parties changed.

Geordie Brown arrived early in 1919 while we were still at Barham. He must have been about thirty then and he stayed with father until he retired. I think he was employed as a groom, but later became an under-chauffeur. He moved to Leslie along with all the house staff. Father took over at Leslie the following outside staff: Walter Ruddiman, head forester, who lived at the forester's lodge; his brother John who lived at the saw mill lodge; I am sure there was a gamekeeper whose name was Herd; McNaughton the head gardener; and I think another gardener and Hastie, the house odd-job man who lived at the Duchess Lodge.

The Ruddimans were both delightful men and remained with us until they retired. McNaughton was a very meticulous man and a good gardener. He came down to the house every morning to see to the flowers in the conservatory which was built on part of the old south wing. When on duty he always wore his bowler hat, and he always prefaced his remarks with, 'Begging your pardon Mister but . . .' Hastie carried all the firewood and coal to the rooms and every other heavy load up those dreadful steep back stairs from the back door. He also looked after the small hydro-electric plant which supplied the light for the house. It must have been about the 1920s that Bell arrived as head chauffeur and Wattie Forsyth as groom.

The 1920s proved to be a period of depression, not least among the farmers, and Father was able to buy back five of the in-by farms. They included two on the south side including the home farm, and three on the north side.

During the next few years we were in turn taught to shoot by the gamekeeper. Douglas was quite a good shot as was Frank, but I was always very poor, and remained so.

Our Christmas and Easter holidays were spent at Leslie but our summer holidays were spent at Glenshirra, so perhaps we should turn that way for a little.

# CHAPTER 4

# Glenshirra

The 1919 Season at Glenshirra was rather a non-starter for me as I was under the charge of Mrs Grier and was not allowed to participate in most of the activities of my brothers. There is one thing I do remember, and that is the ex-army T-Model Ford ambulance which Father had bought as a shooting brake. The control system on these remarkable vehicles was a law unto itself. It had a hand throttle, two pedals and a lever, but how it worked I cannot remember. On one occasion we went to church at Laggan Bridge in it and on returning the engine would not switch off. On investigation it was found that the engine was so hot it fired again automatically.

We did not return to Glenshirra in 1920 as Father was occupied in consolidating the position at Leslie but we did go back every season from 1921 to 1928. The preparations and travel arrangements were quite something. Although the lodge was furnished and had crockery and lamps, it had no electricity or central heating. I think we had to take everything else including linen. Think of it, five children with nannies, a lady's maid, two pantry-maids, two kitchen-maids, two housemaids and two chauffeurs.

The transport available on the establishment to convey all this was obviously not enough, for it consisted of two cars and a shooting brake. This last vehicle was purpose-built on a Fiat chassis. It always seemed to me to be under-powered and had no self-starter or electric light; in fact it only had oil lamps. The front seat could accommodate the driver and two others; behind there were seats

for five more on either side, and a rear door. The sides above seat
level were canvas and could be rolled up but they never were except
for the back ones, which were never down. There was no communication between front and rear. To meet the transport problem a
furniture van was hired, and school trunks, laundry baskets, suitcases and innumerable boxes piled up in the hall. That got rid of
the luggage but there was still a personnel problem. Father drove
one car, Bell the other and Geordie Brown the shooting brake. By
squeezing two into the front of the furniture van the balance were
accommodated with Frank and me in the shooting brake. Although
the journey was only a hundred miles it was a day's journey. The
two cars were rationed together but the shooting brake carried its
own rations as it was considered too slow to make the picnic
on time.

The Great North Road, as it was called in those days, was from
about Struan to Dalwhinnie really only a single track road with
passing places. All this section was on the east side of the railway,
except for a short section just north of Drumochter. On one occasion we had passed under the railway once but on arriving at the
second bridge we found a furniture van jammed under it. After a
consultation with the driver it was decided that we could probably
push him through if we let his rear tyres down. It worked; by this
time others had arrived to help and it was not long before we had
his tyres blown up and him on his way again.

We left the main road at Dalwhinnie, from where on the road
was just gravel. Almost immediately there was a steep hill and it
was touch and go if we in the shooting brake could make the top
without boiling. We turned west just short of Laggan Bridge, and
after another mile or so turned through a gate onto a private road.
Another four miles, over several wooden bridges, brought us to our
destination. The lodge was situated on a small plateau on the south-
east corner of Loch Crunachan, and was almost completely
surrounded by pine trees. The front door was on the east side with
the drawing-room and dining-rooms on the north-west, looking

out over the loch. On the south side was the back door, kitchens and nursery, and a gravel yard on the east side of which were garages, stables and gunroom with a bothy above.

Inside the lodge the rooms were very small with the exception of the drawing-room, dining-room, and the rooms above, which I think must have been added on at some time.

To the east of the lodge and at a lower level was the stalker's house and croft. This house was a very miserable, damp little place and next to it was the bothy for the gillies which consisted of two rooms, one at the back for sleeping in and the front room with an open grate. Neither building had any mod. cons. and water had to be carried from a burn. Out of season, the stalker lived in the lodge and the bothy was unoccupied. To the south of the lodge there was a small hill area, most of which was covered in birch scrub, with some pines on the west. This area usually held some black game and masses of rabbits. There was a right of way which joined the main road at Loch Laggan Hotel. The bulk of the land lay to the north and west of the lodge. The second stalker's house was some six miles to the north, and access was by the old General Wade road. Two miles up this road was General Wade's Old Barracks and Garva Bridge over the Spey. From the stalker's house on, the road was impassable to wheeled vehicles, but it was easily followed on foot over Corrieairack Pass and on to Fort Augustus. The march on the west and north followed the watershed of the Spey.

All the time we were there we had the same stalkers, a father and son called William and Jimmy Wilson. Wilson, as we called the father, was a rugged man but full of fun and we boys adored him. Jimmy lived six miles up the Glen and was newly married: in fact, I think he was single when we were there first in 1919. Jimmy's children were born in this remote spot, without any doctors, of course. He was a very hard working man and managed his croft very well. He had two or three cows and always sold his weaned calves well. Between where we parked the shooting brake and Jimmy's house there was quite a large burn, impassable to motor vehicles. Jimmy paved the ford, so making it passable, and then bought himself a second hand car. This enabled him to take his wife shopping instead of having to leave his order with his father. One of Jimmy's children, a daughter, was named after my sister Clare. Many years later, Mrs Jimmy who was a self-taught artist gave me two watercolours, one of Garva Bridge and one of the lodge, as a wedding present. These now hang in our bedroom at Struy. There were two gillies and a pony man. Geordie Brown was fitted out in plus-fours and so in addition to driving the shooting brake acted as spare pony man.

From 1921 on Father allowed us to participate progressively more and more in the sport. For example, when a guest went to have a shot at the target we were allowed to have a few shots and so gain confidence before being allowed to aim at a live stag.

The grouse were shot over dogs and we enjoyed walking in the line and watching the dogs ranging back and fore. When I was small and the heather long I welcomed a point as it gave me a short rest while the birds were flushed and the shot birds picked up. I remember one occasion when one of the guns was my Uncle Jim Holroyd. It was a very hot day when he suddenly stopped, put down his gun and started to tear open his shirt front. He thrust in his hand and out came a large piece of thermogeen wool.

Even in 1921 Father took me stalking with him, but when we got into a stalk I was left with the gillies. On some occasions we had some very long and cold waits. In 1922 I was out with Father and he suddenly said to me, 'Would you like a shot?'

'Yes,' I whispered, so in I crawled, with Wilson carrying the rifle. The first problem was getting the rifle and myself into a position from which I could see the deer. The next problem was identifying the stag to shoot. Finally, this was done and I drew a bead and fired.

'You have missed it,' said Wilson, and my heart sank. It was all open sights in those days. As it was getting late we had a quick look round and then set off for home with me with my tail between my legs. I was lucky as I was given another chance, and I was successful.

Great was my joy when a few days later another stalking party found my first stag dead in a peat hag, only a few yards from where I had shot at it.

As we grew older we boys were allowed to go out in pairs alone, armed with a .27 rifle looking for roe deer. When Frank and I were about thirteen and fifteen, Michael and Bill Lindsay came to stay. The four of us went out to look for a roe, but we did not see anything, perhaps not surprising with four boys together.

A day or two later the Lindsay boys asked Father if they could go and look for a roe. 'We know where to go, we went with Kay and Frank.'

'All right,' said Father, 'but don't be late back.'

'Yes, Sir, thank you, Sir,' and off they went. They returned in good time looking very pleased with themselves.

'Well, how did you get on?' said Father.

'We got one!'

'Well, what have you done with it?' asked Father. 'The boys usually carry them home if they get one.'

They looked at one another, then said, 'We couldn't, it was much too heavy.'

Someone was found to go back with them to recover their quarry. They had in fact shot a stag which weighed about fourteen stone.

Another sport which we three boys enjoyed was trying to catch pike in the loch. The most usual method was to troll with a spoon bait behind the boat, but another method was to get an empty wine bottle, replace the cork, then attach about a yard of wire trace to it with a triple hook baited with a chunk of venison. If there was time, you just set it loose and watched it. If you were lucky and a pike took, there followed a chase after the bottle. If there was not time for this we would anchor the bottle to a stone, for recovery later.

As there was no electric light, candles were provided for each guest to enable them to find their way to bed. No candle was reissued below about two inches, so Frank and I, who shared a room, used to collect all the short ends and we sometimes had about thirty or more on the mantlepiece in our room. How we did not burn the house down, I don't know.

One season, I think it must have been one of the early ones, Father had engaged a butler called Leishman. He was a very curious man who used to decorate the dining-room table with the most beautiful intricate floral designs. Alas, there came the fatal day when he found us in his pantry. He chased us out with a broom and we dashed out into the yard with him after us. We decided on counter-attack and seized the hose which was used for washing the cars. The result of this encounter was Father receiving Leishman's notice. I think he stayed to the end of the season.

There were one or two burns above Garva Bridge which held quantities of small trout. As far as I can remember, there was only one trout rod between us three boys and we took it in turn to fish, but that did not matter too much as there were plenty of fish and the rod circulated round us quite quickly. We would sometimes come home with fifteen or twenty four-ounce trout which poor Kate was expected to clean and cook. Another pastime was the tennis court, which was situated down near the stalker's house. Unfortunately, more often than not we were driven in by the midges. The other game was 'kick the can'. For those who do not know this ancient game I shall give a short description of it.

An old can was placed in the centre of the gravel area outside the front door. Some sort of lottery then took place to decide who was to be *it*, and another was selected to take the initial kick. As this kick was taken all but *it* ran off and hid. It was the task of *it* to find first the can and bring it back to base and then all the hidden ones. Any one caught before getting back to base became a prisoner. Prisoners could be released by one of the hiders kicking the can while *it* was on search, and rarely did *it* make a full catch. All house guests were expected to join in. As we grew older this game faded in popularity as we took more and more to the field sports.

From about 1926 onwards I was able to drive the shooting brake up the hill road and well do I remember that road. From Garva Bridge to Jimmy's house where we left it there were ninety-three water courses across it which you had to bump into and out. Having parked the vehicle you opened the bonnet, wrapped up the magneto in a piece of oil-silk, then covered the engine with an old carriage rug and then closed the bonnet. All this was in order to get it started; there being no self-starter, it had to be swung. The first season we had this vehicle it quickly became apparent that there was not enough room in the back for four or five men and two or three stag, so Father bought a purpose built trailer to fit behind the brake. When next season came off we set from Leslie with Frank and me sitting on either side at the back. No one had thought about mud wings for the trailer and on our journey we crossed some newly tarred areas and were bombarded by tarry chips. There being no communication between front and rear there was nothing we could do about it. We arrived with faces and heads covered with tar. Next year we had mud wings.

I must mention some of Father's guests as many of them had a considerable influence on my life. First must be J.G.O. Thomson (Jim Thomson). He had been Father's best man and a Cambridge friend. He was a tall, rather delicate man and we all thought him a confirmed bachelor. Suddenly, however, about 1923, he married Eva McAndrew who was young enough to be his daughter. It was a very happy marriage and they had two children. When later on Jim died, Eva became one of the greatest friends of Ursula and me. Uncle John Thomson-Walker was another regular. He was a very interesting man and much liked by the stalkers as he would chat to them on such a wide range of subjects. He used to lecture and demonstrate to medical students at some of the London hospitals. Owing to his love of stalking he started his lectures later than most. When he retired he received a rather unique present of a large silver salver with a crest in the middle from some of his ex-students. The crest looked beautiful; it consisted of a large shield surmounted by a stag's head. When examined in detail you saw that the large subject in the centre of the shield was a heart. The heart was itself divided into quarters, in one of which there was a kidney, in another a liver, in another gall-stones, and I cannot remember what was in the fourth quarter. The stag's antlers were intestines. Perhaps you have guessed that my uncle was a distinguished urological surgeon.

Then there was John Inglis, a Border farmer who had served in the Fife and Forfar Yeo, who eventually married my cousin Cissie Nairn. Another horsy Border farmer and ex-Fife and Forfar was Charles Herdman. He was another who married late in life. He used to ride Father's horses in point to points, and was a very amusing man.

Ian Bruce, a Cambridge friend of Douglas, came one season. He emigrated to Australia and farmed at Orange in New South Wales. After the Second World War I stayed with Ian at Orange and saw him on several of my visits to Australia. Another regular was Dr Dorothy Douglas, a daughter of our family doctor in Cupar.

There is one more whom I will introduce here although she actually joined us in Leslie. Enid Price, a cousin of my mother's from Canada, came to stay for a fortnight and stayed eighteen months. She returned to Canada, married and had several children many of whom have visited us. Enid and I still correspond.

The Glenshirra years, covering those formative years from prep. school to university, sowed in me a love for the hill and the chase. I shot my first stag in 1922 and my last one in 1992, having only missed six seasons during that period, four of which were the war years and on the other two I had a broken leg. Is this a record?

# CHAPTER 5

# Trains and Shrewsbury

Few people today appreciate how much our lives were affected by the railways. There were very, very few cars and no lorries, except horse drawn ones, so I think they deserve a mention here. Until after the end of the first world war there were a great number of railway companies, each servicing a relatively small area: for instance, in Scotland, I can remember the Highland Railway, the West Highland, the North British, the Caledonian and I am sure there were some more. Each company had its own colour scheme for its rolling stock and in particular for its engines. The most spectacular colour scheme I can remember was the Caledonian, whose engines were painted a bright sky blue, and that funny dome which stuck up between the funnel and the cab was highly polished brass.

Most of the passenger coaches were non-corridor, with compartments the full width of the coach. They had a bench seat on either side which in the case of 3rd class were not very comfortable. The doors could not be opened from inside; you had to open the window and put your hand out. The windows were raised and lowered by a leather strap. Long distance trains all had corridors. They were heated by steam from the engine, so if you boarded at a terminus before the engine had been coupled up you were very cold. I think the brakes were also operated by steam.

The main interest to all small boys was the engines. Each one had to have its own coal and water supply and the usual crew was two, the driver and the fireman. Engines came in a variety of shapes and sizes and were usually identified by the number of wheels they had. For example the largest usually were 4–6–0: that meant they had four wheels on the front bogie, six driving wheels and nothing behind.

The other distinguishing feature was the tender. Long distance engines all had tenders which carried coal and water, while shunting engines had saddle tanks for water and small self contained bunkers for coal. I must not forget the goods trains which carried so much of the country's freight. A goods wagon was short, and had buffers and a hook and two links of chain at each end. Most were open but many were covered. The sorting out of goods wagons and making them up into trains was a very complicated and skilled business and took place in marshalling yards. As the wagons had no brakes their speed was limited so that when they stopped the driver stopped and each wagon then bumped into the one in front. It was a very familiar noise hearing the goods trains stopping and starting.

Having been sent to a prep. school in Brighton and a public school in Shrewsbury we soon became experienced travellers.

When I first went to Cottesmore I was twelve and thought myself quite grown up and quite confident. If I had been on my own and not with a younger brother I might have been a little less confident. We were taken to Kirkcaldy station, where a through ticket for Brighton was bought, and we were given ten shillings travelling money. Our trunks were labelled Kings Cross but we still had to recover them at Waverley and see them onto the London train. That porter had to be tipped, sixpence I expect. We carried our lunch, and on arrival at Kings Cross we found a porter, retrieved our luggage and then found a taxi. One more porter to tip. The taxi took us to Victoria where he was paid off and a porter found to convey our luggage to the Brighton train. This meant one more porter to tip, but in spite of having paid the taxi five shillings we usually had a few pence to buy something from the book-stall. The journeys to Shrewsbury, if we started from Kirkcaldy, required a change of station in Edinburgh from Waverley to Princes Street

Station. We then had to change at Crewe where we had a long wait. When we started from Glenshirra we caught the night train for London at Kingussie. We got out at Crewe about one o'clock in the morning and had a two hour wait for the next train.

Sending parcels by train was quite a common thing. You took your package to the station labelled for its final destination and you paid the charge. On arrival at this station, if you lived in a town it would be delivered to you by horse lorry. If you lived in the country you were sent a postcard telling you to collect it. If you required something urgently you could telephone the shop and ask them to put it on a specific train which you then met.

While on the subject of travel to school I must cover my journey to Shrewsbury during the 1926 general strike. A few trains were operating manned by volunteer crews made up of university students and others. There were no trains from Scotland South. The seamen had not gone on strike but the dockers had. The Dundee, Perth and London coastal steamer was sailing from Dundee over the weekend for London, so David Walker and I booked two berths out of the very few that they had. There was no cargo on board and we had a terribly rough passage, but we arrived in London early on Monday morning. The trip had been so rough that the steward poured water on the tablecloth to stop the plates slipping off the tables. We were travelling light and I don't remember how we got from the docks to Euston, where we went in search of a train. It was still quite early when we found one going in the right direction, so we boarded it. It travelled very slowly and stopped at every station and we must have eventually arrived back at school very late.

I do not remember my actual arrival at Mr Moore's House, Shrewsbury, probably because I just tagged along behind Douglas and had nothing to worry about. However, after the comforts of Cottesmore the conditions were spartan. Moore's House was two semi-detached three-storey and basement houses. The boys occupied one and Mr Moore the other. I do not remember how many boys there were but we were very tightly squeezed in. We lived in communal studies, with about ten or twelve boys to each. High-backed desks were arranged all round the walls in such a way that no two boys shared a chair space. You were allotted a desk for the term in which you kept all your possessions and under which you kept your tuck box. In the centre, with its back to the fire, there was a flat-topped desk and a table. As a new boy you sat nearest the door, the coldest spot. As the years passed you progressed nearer and nearer to the fire until, if you were lucky, you became a house monitor and had the flat-topped desk. The house monitors were responsible for house and study discipline and had considerable power, including the right to beat boys. For your first two years you were a dowel (in Greek, a slave). If a monitor shouted 'Dowel!' all the dowels had to rush to him and the last to arrive got the job. Some of the house monitors were also school monitors and had responsibilities outside the house.

Our house had no central heating and was always very cold unless you had a desk near the fire. There was a very limited domestic hot water supply and hot baths were restricted to one a fortnight in winter and none in summer. A cold shower was all you had to wash in after games. The lavatories were located outside and in severe weather a coke brazier was provided to prevent a freeze up. The food was very basic and very monotonous; we augmented it from our tuck boxes. There was also a school shop where you could buy sweets and other oddments. At week-ends they served hot meals. We were given £5 a term for this expenditure.

I cannot remember the exact timings of the daily routine, but it was approximately as follows. Bell at seven o'clock, cold bath, dress, pick up books and cap and proceed to school for first lesson. Return for breakfast, via chapel, about nine and back to school about 9.45 till lunch at 2 p.m. In the winter terms we played games after lunch and went back to school from four to six o'clock and then back for tea (supper), then prep. before bed at ten o'clock.

Most of the classrooms were in one large three-storey block, but there was also a science building. Behind the main school building and at the bottom of a steep bank was the river Severn and the boat houses. At the boat-house there was a hand-operated ferry attached to a wire hawser across the river. We were not allowed across without permission. I was no good at football or cricket so, being a light-weight, was seized as a cox. This did not mean that I escaped the school runs or the cold and muddy practice games. I used to enjoy playing fives, although I was not much good.

In one of my early years I caught mumps and was sent to the sanitarium along with others. We quickly got better but were kept in quarantine. During this period we were permitted to go for walks up a country road which passed behind the San. We were not allowed to go the other way into the town, but some of us were caught doing just that. Next day we were walking in the right direction when we met the Headmaster, Canon Sawyer. He spoke to us about our misdemeanour and then told us to bend over and we each got a few whacks across the bottom. When we were vertical again he said, 'I think all the more of you for that, the adventurous spirit of youth,' and we all walked home together. Canon Sawyer was a very short and extremely round little man, but a great sport.

My career as a cox progressed quite well and I coxed the school second eight and just failed to cox that famous Shrewsbury eight which won the Ladies' Plate at Henley. Eventually I got too heavy and took to rowing, something which stood me in good stead later.

During the week we wore blue suits, white shirt with white stiff collar, and black tie. On Sunday we wore morning suits and top hats.

There was a nice chapel situated between the main school build-ing and the science building. We attended once every morning and twice on Sunday. I enjoyed the services.

I think I must be a bit of a loner as I made no lasting friends at school. One thing I did do was to join the OTC. With my experience at Glenshirra I quickly found myself in the shooting eight and went to Bisley, which was good experience and fun.

I may be wrong, but I can only remember my parents visiting Shrewsbury once while I was there. It did not make much difference whether your parents came or not, as the restrictions on what you could do were so limiting: for instance you had to be back in school quite early each evening, leaving your parents kicking their heels. There were no nights away, not even at half term.

I was no scholar but just about managed to keep my place in my age group. I managed to drag myself through my public school years without trouble and without distinction. I did not even manage to become a house monitor. I failed to get a school certificate so had to go to Cambridge to sit my entrance exam there. Once again I was fortunate as my brother Douglas found me a bed in his digs and showed me the ropes. This was 1927 and, by another miracle, I passed this exam too.

# CHAPTER 6

# Back at Leslie

Back at Leslie many things were happening I cannot remember the exact dates on which everything happened but they will have been between 1921 and 1930.

There is one date which I do remember: that is 14 November 1924, when my youngest sister Margaret was born. She was so much younger than us boys that she hardly seemed like a sister. She was seven years younger than Clare, her nearest sister, and sixteen years younger than me. However, over the years that gap seems to have narrowed.

Another thing which happened over these years was the increase in the staff, both inside and outside. Inside, the staff rose to: a housekeeper, a butler, a footman and a table-maid. A lady's maid; two in the nursery; three house-maids; three in the kitchen; and of course Hastie.

Outside there were three in the garden; two foresters; two chauffeurs; two grooms; and later an ex-Weeden army staff sergeant to break the young horses and a stud groom and farm staff at the home farm. Oh! I have forgotten the gamekeeper. Quite an army.

During this period I, along with my brothers, was passing through those vital teenage years when you not only grow physically but mature mentally.

One of the first things which made a considerable difference to my life was my purchase, with I am sure a lot of assistance, of my first bicycle which came from Dalls of Ladybank. This machine, which I kept till I left Cambridge, enabled me to get around the estate and especially to the home farm in a very short time. South Parks, as the home farm was called, was some half mile from the house and was often visited by me before breakfast. On gaining possession of the farm my father engaged McKenzie as farm manager and one of his first duties was to acquire dairy cows to supply the big house with milk and butter and quite a lot must have been required to feed the army.

My father had many interests as well as his duties as joint managing director with his brother of the family linoleum business. He was on the County Council, and interested in politics. From the recreational point of view his primary interest was hunting and horses, but of course he also loved his deer stalking, fishing and to a lesser extent covert shooting. With a father with such wide interests it gave us every opportunity to gain knowledge of country life and field sports. I think it must have been in 1927 that my father received a knighthood. This created problems, particularly for my mother who became Lady Nairn. As there were already two other Lady Nairns confusion began to appear. There was little problem with my grandmother; the trouble lay between the two sisters-in-law who were both engaged in social and charitable work. Father therefore decided to change our name to Spencer-Nairn. My father was already christened Spencer, his mother's maiden name, and he was known by that name. The change took place in 1928, while I was at Cambridge.

I think Father must have acquired his first post-war hunter very soon after arriving at Leslie and I have no doubt it was followed by a second one very soon after. Hunting from Leslie was quite a performance as Leslie was outside the area hunted by the Fife Fox Hounds and it was necessary to go on by train as there were no motor horse boxes in those days. The drill was to notify the railway company twenty-four hours before, naming the station you wished to entrain and where you wished to go to. This usually meant being at Markinch station about 8 a.m. and more often than not you had a few miles to hack on after leaving the train. It also meant that you had to be back at the re-embarkation station by a fixed time. It was often between seven and eight o'clock before the horses were back at the stables.

It was also about this time that Father became interested in the breeding of hunters and the work of the Hunters' Improvement Society. The HIS encouraged an individual or a group of individuals to sponsor a thoroughbred stallion to travel the country for the use of local persons with suitable mares. Father agreed to do just this and an approved stallion was selected and operated from Leslie stable with Father supplying the stud groom to lead it. The next move was the building of a range of boxes at South Parks, and the horse breeding activities were transferred up there.

Every winter the HIS held a show at Islington Hall in London at which stallions competed for premiums and were approved as suitable to travel. Stallions in Scotland did not have to travel to London but were inspected by an HIS inspector, who was for many years Colonel King whom we got to know very well. After the facilities were ready at South Parks Father bought a stallion whom he kept for three or four years and then replaced. As I grew older I got quite involved in helping Father in this venture.

While we were at school Father did not supply any ponies for us to ride, but as we got bigger we were allowed to ride exercise on his hunters. We received little or no riding instruction and Mother's lack of interest did not help. As young horses began to appear from South Parks, Father started looking for someone to school them. Through the good offices of Harry Hutchison, who was commandant of the Army School of Equitation at Weedon, he engaged Tom Brown who had been a sergeant instructor there. Tom Brown's arrival on the scene gave us a wonderful opportunity to learn to ride properly. I benefited enormously.

Covert shooting was another activity which I struggled to master but with little success. Although I maintained an interest I never became an addict.

My mother enjoyed what can only be described as country house tennis. There was a grass lawn at Leslie which was wide enough but only just long enough for a court. It was equipped and marked out but proved to be too soft and too short. As we boys were becoming more and more interested, it was decided that a hard court would be more suitable for the Scottish climate: the problem was where to put it. It was deemed to be too unsightly a thing to be seen from the windows of the house which made finding a site very difficult. Eventually one was found in the corner of the Lilly Park some 250 yards from the house and behind some trees and rhododendron bushes. One was duly built there and a suitable wooden tennis house erected. It was used quite a lot right up to the Second World War.

The Sunday afternoon tennis parties were quite something. If you were a male you dressed in long white trousers, white shirt, and jacket or blazer, not forgetting the silk scarf round your neck. The blazer and scarf were removed for play but on the arrival of tea they were put on again. The butler and footman carried the tea all the way from the house and a spread was laid out. Play was allowed to continue during tea and tea was taken in shifts. The court was one of those red ash ones which made your long white trousers filthy, and necessitated their being cleaned every time you played. However we had a lot of fun.

Stowed away at the back of the garage there was an old Sunbeam motor-bike, which Father had used during the war. It was a terrifically heavy machine which you had to heave up onto its stand by the carrier. It had a board either side for your feet and shields to protect you from the mud. There were two levers on the right side: one was the throttle and the other the ignition. There were no twist grips in those days. It had a crash gear-box and required double declutching and the hand throttle to operate so it was quite difficult to learn to drive. However, as its back wheel was off the ground when it was sitting on its stand you could practise all the motions in that position. Who sorted it out, I don't remember. However, when it was pronounced to be in running order I bought a motor-bike driving licence for which you became eligible at fourteen. As I was small and not very strong I found it too much to handle, but I did go all the way to Rankeilour and back on it one day. I think I learnt to drive a car at Glenshirra and was quite able to drive the shooting brake up and down the General Wade road by the time I was sixteen. You had to be eighteen before you could get a licence to drive a car, but there were no driving tests.

From time to time during our school days Father would take one or two of us boys down to the factory in Kirkcaldy on a Saturday morning. There we were handed over to some factory manager who would take us round his area of responsibility. By this means we were introduced to the factory scene and smells.

In those early days we grew up in the lap of luxury. I never had to make my bed; that was done first by a nanny and later by a house-maid. My clothes were looked after, first by a nanny, then by a house-maid and finally by the footman who acted as valet to me. We changed for dinner every night and my dinner jacket was laid out. All I had to do was strip off and have my bath, leaving everything on the floor; then when I came up to bed all was tidy and my pyjamas were laid out. In the morning when I was called I was asked what clothes I required and they were produced. If I was going away for a night all I had to do was to say what I required and it would be packed for me. If I was going by train a car was ordered to be at the door at the appropriate time and I would saunter into the hall then where I found the footman with my bag, hat, coat and umbrella. If I was going by car the procedure was the same except that my car would be left at the door. It all seemed so simple and so natural.

Now a word about some of the most memorable members of the staff. First there was Kate Whitehead who was cook for most of the twenties. She spoilt us and would always produce all the things we liked when we were home on holiday. Then there was Plumb who came as butler sometime during the twenties and stayed until the Second World War. He was a large, jovial man and hailed from East

Anglia where his father had been a policeman. His elder brother was a regular soldier and rose to become Captain Plumb, Equitation Officer in the Life Guards. Plumb was quite a character and became very well known to my parents' house guests. He was a great favourite of my sisters; he was also a keen fisherman and when at the various shooting lodges he could be seen of an afternoon off fishing, dressed in immaculate plus-fours and a trilby hat. I don't remember any of the nannies who looked after me, but I do remember nanny Frances who looked after my elder sisters. When they grew out of the nursery she left and emigrated to Australia, where I visited her on several occasions when over there on business. Mary McNaughton, the second daughter of the head gardener, came as nanny to Margaret and eventually went on to my brother Douglas to look after his children. Her elder sister had married Jim Barclay, the local grocer, who was a most amusing man and was very good to us: no doubt the account helped. Ursula and I kept in touch with Lizzie until she died in her nineties.

When enumerating the total staff earlier I forgot Duncan, one of the garden staff, amongst whose duties was the garden horse. Every large garden had a garden horse which pulled the garden cart and the mowing machine. There were no motor mowers. In fact, I think we went on using the horse-drawn mower for the large front lawn well after motor mowers were available. Another member of the garden staff was Bob Gordon, who started straight from school as an apprentice. He eventually married Chrissie Smith who was our (Ursula and my) first house-maid.

Head of the stable staff was Bell, who had been a coachman and knew about horses, but now was also head chauffeur. He was a short thick man with a round open face. He was most respectful and always touched his cap before and after speaking to you. He was good at his job and was prepared to take responsibility for all the stable and garage staff. Geordie Brown whom I have already mentioned was second chauffeur and general worker. Next came Wattie Fordyce, the groom, typically bow-legged, small and cheery.

When we started to grow up and the horse numbers grew he was joined by Willie Herd, the younger brother of the stud groom at South Parks. Then there was Tom Brown whom I have already mentioned.

When we came to Leslie, Father took over the gamekeeper whose name was also Herd. I cannot remember what happened to him, but his successor was called Hadden. I have already mentioned the two Rudimans, the foresters. In time they both died and were replaced by two other brothers, Henry and Wattie McLean.

# CHAPTER 7

# Cambridge

Nineteen twenty-seven was a watershed in my life. I managed to get through the exam for Cambridge and was billed to join my brother Douglas at Trinity Hall in October. I replaced my motor cycle licence with a full licence which, believe it or not, covered all vehicles including steam rollers. My parents kitted me out with a dinner jacket and evening tail coat, all of which I can still wear today. Up till then my only party dress had been a kilt. But a much more important thing happened: Father made me financially independent.

I was taken to father's private office where I was given a note book in which there were recorded a list of investments, showing the sum invested in each holding and dividend payment dates. I was given a simple double-entry cash book and shown how to operate it, and finally I had to sign a specimen signature form and was told that I would soon receive from the Bank of Scotland, 30 Bishopsgate, London, a bank book and a cheque book. I was told that from now on I was financially responsible for all my requirements, including university fees, clothes, travel, etc. I was also allowed to smoke if I wished; there was no lung cancer scare, it was never heard of.

On receipt of my bank book I discovered that a small cash balance had been deposited for me to give me a start. I started my financial planning very carefully, determined to show that I could manage my own affairs. What good training it was and I was very grateful to my father.

I don't remember how I travelled to Cambridge or how my luggage, including my bicycle, got there but we all did. I was allotted a room in college on N staircase; I was lucky as several freshmen did not get a room in college. We lived in luxury with a study and bedroom, with a gyp and bedder to look after us. The gyps and bedders looked after students on two staircases. My first gyp was called Laing and had been a gyp when my father was up. We freshmen were assembled in Hall and told of the rules and regulations governing university life, after which a photograph was taken. The Rev. Chase was my college tutor, but he was not responsible for my studies. I can remember remarkably little about the educational side of my university life, other than that I managed to scrape through first time on each exam occasion.

At Trinity Hall there was a passage between the first court and the inner court, on one side of which was the dining hall and on the other the kitchens. The walls of this passage were covered with notice boards where were posted all notices of college activities, including sport and recreation. There were sheets asking for volunteers and I put my name down on the rowing list where there were one or two who had come from rowing schools like Eton and Shrewsbury, but the bulk had no previous experience.

The dining hall was a typical medieval building, long, narrow, oak panelled to approximately seven feet with tall windows above. At the far end there was a raised area where the dons dined. It had a high vaulted roof. On each side there was a fixed bench seat in front of which there was a long refectory table and then a movable bench. We were served our meals by the gyps. The procedure was to study the menu which was posted at the door, then tick your name off as present. You could order special dishes if you wished and any drinks from beer to port.

The kitchen staff was all male and they still used all the old copper pots, which were beautifully kept. I gather that when the war came and women replaced the men all these copper pots had to go as they were too heavy for them. The kitchens and cellar were under a gentleman called Harvey and the head chef was called Munnings. They were responsible to the bursar who in turn was responsible to the Master and Fellows for the domestic running of the college.

You could order meals to be sent up to your rooms and even out to your digs if you lived out of college. If you wished a very special meal for any reason you conferred with Harvey and Munnings on the menu. They were wonderful and made you feel that you really did know something about the subject when in reality they were making the decisions. All these special meals had to be paid for and were debited to your account. This restricted the occasions say to birthdays or when some friend came to see you from outside the university and you wished to entertain him in your rooms. Most of the sporting clubs and societies had annual dinners and there was a common-room where these dinners could be held.

Discipline was maintained within the college by the college authorities and outside the college by the proctors. One was not supposed to be out after a certain hour without a gown on. To enforce this the proctors, dressed in gown and mortar board and supported by two bullers dressed in tails and with a top hat, patrolled the streets. It was the duty of the bullers to catch you and bring you before the proctor. He took your name and college and you usually received a fine.

Entry to colleges was through a door or gate and was supervised by the college porters. The head porter at the Hall when I was up was Albert Pamplin and the deputy was Grant; both these characters had been porters when my father was up. Albert Pamplin along with Bill Beatie the hairdresser in Jesus Lane had a very nice partridge shoot at Six Mile Bottom. Bill Beatie was another of these characters only to be found in Cambridge; he was seldom to be found in his shop on days when there was a race meeting at Newmarket.

The Trinity Hall boat house was next door to the University boat house. I don't remember how the freshmen were sorted out but I soon found myself slogging away on a fixed seat eight. I think it was through rowing that I first made contact with Mike Harrison and we quickly became friends. That first term was spent in practice and in the hope of getting a place in one of the Lent boats.

The ground floor of the boat house was given over to the storage of boats but upstairs there were three changing rooms, one for the freshmen and novices, the second for the second boat crews and the other for the first boat and officials. When we changed for rowing we hung our clothes up on a peg without a thought for security and nothing ever went missing. Each changing room had its own shower and lots of hot water. This provided us with a daily hot shower which was a great boon as baths in college were a problem and often required a long walk outside.

I think it was during this, my first term, that I discovered the existence of the Senior Officers Training Corps and that amongst the units represented was a cavalry squadron. I thought it would be fun so I put my name down to join next term, and went home for Christmas resolved to return with a pair of breeches, short boots and leggings. I rode quite a bit during the holidays, but I don't remember if I went hunting or not.

I returned to Cambridge early in January to start serious training for the Lent races. I was fortunate in gaining bow position in the second boat. This crew turned out to be rather a good one and we went up four places and won our oars.

Through the good offices of someone I became a member of the Pit Club. This was a social and dining club situated in Jesus Lane and about halfway between the Hall and the Boat Club. It proved to be a very handy place for me, where I could get lunch and read the papers. It was also a place where one could meet people from other colleges.

Life became very routine without much of interest to record and it was not long before another holiday had come and gone and we were back training for the May races. After our triumph in the Lents I got a place in the second May boat. I think we made a bump

Trinity Hall oarsmen relaxing.

or two. It was during this term that the entries had to be made for Henley Royal Regatta and the crews chosen. I was very surprised to see my name on the list as spare man and that I would have the opportunity to go as a member of the Hall party. The boat club was run by a captain and secretary, the former of which was usually a third year student and the latter a second year student. As another surprise, I was asked if I would be prepared for my name to be put forward as secretary to take over from Harold Elworthy a very popular New Zealander. In due course I was elected and Robin Ellis, who had stroked Cambridge to victory, was elected captain but we did not take over till the October term. To go to Henley, even as a spare man, in one's first year was a great privilege. There were two of us and all we had to do was to keep fit by rowing in a pair for about half an hour each morning, after which we could enjoy the regatta. It was a wonderful end to my first year at Cambridge.

In August the family returned to Glenshirra as usual for what turned out to be our last season there, and I was able to enjoy it to the full as I did not have to return to Cambridge until 10 October.

My election as secretary of the boat club had a profound effect on my life at the Hall. First, it meant another year in college as the captain and secretary were allotted rooms opposite one another on the first floor of M staircase. These were two of the nicest rooms in college and the boat club was the only sport whose officials had this privilege. Chalendler was our gyp here, and he too had been a gyp in my father's day; he was also a buller.

The duties of the secretary were quite time-consuming and meant that I had to plan my working day in more detail. Working with the captain, I had the daily task of keeping in touch with each boat coach and then putting up on the notice board before dinner the crews and practice times each day. Should a coach or an oar not be available they notified me and I had to find substitutes. Quite often we were able to obtain the services of Old Hall men to come and coach, but I had to write and ask them. Another task was to make the entries for any regattas the captain wished to enter for. On some occasions this meant finding accommodation. So one had to go and find landladies and bargain with them. Henley and Putney were the only places where I was involved. During all this time I was rowing myself, first in the first Lent boat and then in the Mays. One other job was organising the Trinity Hall Boat Club Ball. There was a committee who made decisions and then left it to the secretary to implement them. I really enjoyed my year as secretary. I learnt a lot and gained a lot of confidence and I also made a lot of friends, both amongst old Hall men and amongst the undergraduates.

Another thing which made a big difference to my life was the acquisition of a car. Father had bought a car for Douglas in his second year so I was fairly confident he would do the same for me. I went back in October without one but I learnt that Father was to be in London for some meeting when the motor show was to be on at Olympia, so I arranged to meet him and go to it. We wandered around for a time and were looking at a Riley 9 when the salesman said, 'We have a nice two seater out in the street which is available for immediate delivery,' so out to the street we went. It looked quite a nice looking little job and I thought, well, a bird in the hand is worth two in the bush, so I persuaded Father that it would suit me very well, and it was bought there and then. A telephone call to Kirkcaldy fixed the insurance and I was ready to set off for Cambridge. That was a very slow journey as it had to be run in for the first five hundred miles at 30 m.p.h. It was a two-seater with a dickie seat behind and outside the hood. It only had two-wheel brakes, but it did have a windscreen wiper driven off the carburettor. The trouble with this sort was that when you put your foot down the wiper stopped and when you took it off again it started again. We were not allowed to keep our cars outside the college for more than a few minutes so I garaged mine with a Mr Birch who was very nice and did not charge too much.

Henley was even more fun that year, although I had all the digs etc. to deal with, as I knew so many more people. We were entered in the Ladies' Plate but Robin Ellis was not rowing in the Hall boat as he was rowing for Leander in the Grand. We got through one or two rounds. We had been coached in the Mays by Tony Miller, one of the identical twins who had been up a year or two before. Another old Hall man whom I must mention was Basil Henderson. He went out of his way to ensure that we had badges for the enclosure and were not without adequate refreshment.

Harold Elworthy, from whom I took over, was going down and returning to New Zealand. He said, 'I must see Scotland before I leave,' so I invited him to come and spend a night with us. Tony Miller said, 'Why not come to us at Knutsford on your way north?' so this was arranged. Once the regatta was over, off we set and arrived at the Old Court House in good time to change for dinner. Father Miller was a great big man and we had a very jolly evening. Next morning after breakfast our bags were all packed and ready for our continuing journey. We arrived at Leslie House just in time to change for dinner. I showed Harold where to report when changed and rushed to get myself ready. I got down before Harold and was chatting to my parents when in walked Harold looking like Charlie Chaplin; his dinner jacket was obviously sizes too big for him. Poor Harold did not know what to say. The Millers' butler had packed father Miller's dinner jacket!

# CHAPTER 8

# Kintail and Cambridge

During the last few years at Glenshirra my mother used to complain that for the ladies it was a boring place, and unless they stalked that was true. Father therefore sought out another place where there were alternative things for the ladies to do, and he found the almost perfect answer, Kintail. Kintail provided both good stalking and sea fishing from a powerful motor yacht. It had recently belonged to a Mr Edwards who had just died, leaving it to Inverness Infirmary. They were letting it for one season while they decided what to do with it. It eventually became the property of the National Trust.

The journey to Kintail was very much longer than to Glenshirra. In fact we passed Laggan Bridge and continued on past Loch Laggan and Roy Bridge to Spean Bridge where we turned right towards Fort Augustus, turning off at Invergarry for Tom Down then north for Glen Shiel at the west end of which was Loch Duich. Kintail Lodge was situated about the centre of the east end of the loch and had magnificent views. The public road passed between the loch and the house, but the traffic was so light it did not matter too much.

All supplies had to come from Kyle of Lochalsh. To get there by road you continued round the north side of the loch and crossed Dornie ferry. This was quite a long trip as well as being a very slow one. The alternative was to go by sea. In the yacht it took about forty-five minutes if you were in a hurry. It was quite a large boat with cabins for the crew and I think four other berths; there was also a cabin in which you could feed. It was powered by two large Stirling petrol engines which drank petrol. There was a crew of two. Gillies the skipper was a delightful elderly man who came from Plockton and really knew the district well. John McRae was the engineer; he too was nice but very quiet. When we went shopping in Kyle we filled up with petrol which usually meant a 40-gallon drum. My mother, my sisters and various lady guests very much enjoyed the yacht, and kept the lodge supplied with fish.

The deer forest had the reputation of being the steepest in Scotland, and included the well known five sisters of Kintail: I believe they were all over 3,000 ft. The head stalker was called McRae. The usual plan was to spy the ground from the bottom and then, having spotted your deer, plan a route by which you could get above them. This meant a long climb from near sea level to nearly 3,000 ft. Having got above them you did not crawl but slid in on your bottom and shot off your knee. There were some places where it was too steep to shoot as the beast would have rolled to the bottom. When dragging it, it was one man in front and two behind to stop the stag over-running the front man. Having spent the year rowing I was in perfect condition for this form of stalking and really enjoyed myself.

When the time came for me to return to Cambridge in my little Riley I knew it would take me two days so I started early before the sun was up. It was one of those lovely mornings with all the cobwebs covered in dew. Then suddenly the sun popped over the horizon in front of me, all the cobwebs turned pink, and, to crown it all, there was a stag standing on the road in front of me.

Early in the May term I realised that I would have to find digs for my last year and as Douglas had been very happy at Causeway House with Mrs Ripley I went to see her. The answer I got was, 'Another Mr Nairn, that would be nice.' So that was that. Causeway House was on the corner of Maid's Causeway and opposite Parker's Piece, beyond which was the river and the boat houses, so it was very convenient for me.

The Ripleys were a wonderful family. There was the mother who ran the house, the father who was a plumber and a daughter who worked in a chemist's shop. In addition there was Tiger, a collie dog and Jeff, Madge's boyfriend. Mrs Ripley was a sort of mother to all her students and looked after us very well. The family lived in the basement while we occupied the upper rooms. We were given breakfast but no other meals, though if ever you came in late she would offer you a cup of tea or even a scrambled egg. This would usually be served in her kitchen and many a happy evening we spent chatting there. The father's plumbing business was controlled through a large Boots diary; each job as it arose was entered in this book and he completed them in strict rotation. In the same way he sent his bills out as cash was required, also in strict rotation. I don't remember seeing any other form of accounting. There was one problem which I think ought to be recorded. There was only one bath in the house, the water for which was heated by a geyser and it took hours to fill a bath. We prevailed on the father, who after all was a plumber, to install a hot water boiler and this was to be done during the vacation. When we returned, of course it was not finished. Quite soon, however, father announced that all was finished and that the fire could be lit. This was planned for the evening when Dad was home from his other work. I think all the residents were present that evening. All seemed to be going splendidly till suddenly boiling water came cascading down the stair. Dad had failed to put the expansion pipe through the roof and with all the stoking the water had boiled. 'You go and tell him what's wrong, Mr Nairn,' said Mrs Ripley. 'He will listen to you.' It wasn't a difficult problem to correct and in a few days all was well.

My companions in Causeway House were Mike Harrison, Mike Gutteridge and one other. I suggested that the Ripleys should visit us at Leslie while on their holiday. This they did and when they arrived, Mrs Ripley's first remark was, 'Oh! Mr Nairn, you did not tell us that you lived in a big house like this.' What happy days those were.

As I now had no secretarial duties I had more time for other things. Having failed to get my crescent (colours) the previous year I was still eligible for the Lents and was rowing in the first Lent boat, which meant a six-day week on the river. The week-ends became rather special. On one occasion, four of us were walking down King's Street on our way to the river when we saw a bicycle made for four outside a shop. We were looking at it when the salesman said, 'Like to have a go with it?' so we hired it for the following Sunday. When we arrived to collect it on Sunday the chap asked if any of us had ridden a tandem. We said no. He pointed out that there was no free wheel and suggested that we put our hands on the shoulders of the man in front, and not on the handle-bars. We drew lots for seating order and I drew the front seat. All went well and we sped off towards Ely. After a while I found the pressure of three heavy men almost too much for my arms; however, we made the fifteen miles to Ely within the hour. After a leisurely lunch we set off for home. After a mile or so, Nick Harris said, 'I have left my gloves behind.' We stopped and sent him back by himself to recover them. What a comical sight he was with three empty seats and all the pedals going round. I have never seen another four-seated bicycle.

Mike and I sometimes went to the Wash bird watching, and on one occasion we went sailing on the Broads.

I mentioned earlier that I had joined the cavalry squadron of the senior OTC. Parades were held at 6.30 a.m. at the Kings Street stables. When it was dark they were confined to the riding school which was lit. There was an officer in charge but as he rarely appeared except when it was daylight, all the instruction was left to SSM Brodie. There was an enclosed jumping lane down one side of the school. One of SSM Brodie's joys was to get us all mounted bareback and then put us through a prolonged period of drill at the trot which was very tiring and then he would finish up by saying, 'Fold your arms and down the lane.'

The other drill I remember was saddling up and mounting. Being the army, it was, of course, done to a strict routine. The bridles were relatively simple, but not so the saddle. First your blanket which went under the saddle had to be folded exactly the right way and then put on the horse's back with the rough edges to the near and rear. You then put the saddle on with the rifle bucket on the off-side. A rolled up groundsheet was strapped to the back of the saddle and a feed bag to the front and I think there were some other things which I have forgotten. The mounting procedure was something like this. You started standing facing forward with your rifle. On the command to mount you turned to face the rear, then, with the reins in your left hand, you swung your rifle over the horse and put it into your left hand, you then put your left foot in the stirrup, seized the back of the saddle with your right hand and sprang up and stood in your stirrup before swinging your right leg over and sitting down in the saddle. Next you seized the rifle by the small of the butt and, standing in the saddle, swung your right arm up and back high enough to get the muzzle into the bucket.

In the summer we rode out to a piece of waste ground where we practised mounted drill. Drill was based on a section of four. If there was to be dismounted action number two remained mounted and took over all the horses. Our officer used to enjoy saying, 'Lead horses follow me,' and off he would go at the gallop and over a small ditch. If you were lucky and your four horses came from the same stable you might get over, but more often than not chaos followed. I regretted not going to annual camp but it always clashed with Henley. However, I did receive my certificate B which entitled me to a commission in the TA.

Towards the end of December 1929 Mike Harrison, Howson Devitt and I decided that we would go to the Varsity rugger match at Twickenham and to the Aula Club dinner afterwards. Howson invited us to his home in Cadogan Gardens to change. We had just arrived and were standing in the hall when his young twin sisters came down the stair. It was their seventeenth birthday and they were being taken out to dinner and to the House of Commons. We said, 'How do you do?' and parted. Six years later Mike and I each married one of the twins. I don't remember who won the rugger match.

Christmas came and went as did the Lent races, and it was time to go home again. I do remember thinking that I could get home in a day if I caught the Queensferry ferry and did not have to go round by Stirling. My problem was that there was no bridge east of Stirling and the Queensferry boat only sailed when there was sufficient water. I got someone to check on the tides for me and left in good time to catch the boat. I arrived in good time and waited for the boat to come over from the north side. As it approached the pier it ran on the rocks and as the tide was falling it was going to have to stay there until next high tide. There was nothing for it but to get back into the car and set off for Stirling. This added seventy miles to my journey. So much for all my careful planning.

Back in Cambridge I managed to get a place in the first May boat and got my crescent, which pleased me very much after all the time I had given to the boat club.

One evening I was driving back into Cambridge on Huntingdon road with John Close, an army officer and fellow student, with me. We came up behind a light lorry stacked high with flower boxes which overlapped the side of the lorry by about a foot. I was just about to overtake it when it swerved right across in front of me. It pushed me right into a tree which was growing on the pavement. I was unhurt but John had a cut on his knee from hitting the dashboard. Someone called an ambulance so we both went into the hospital. John got his leg patched up but said that he had a pain in his tummy. They kept him in and next day removed his appendix. The poor little Riley was a write off. I was charged, as every undergraduate always was, but I got off as I was able to prove that it was impossible for a hand signal to be seen with the load of boxes the man had on the lorry. There were no light signals on cars.

I don't know who organised it but I found myself in a party for the Trinity Hall Boat Club Ball which included the Devitt twins. I

May Week 1930.

was delighted as they looked rather an attractive pair. The Ball went well and we had a lot of fun. I think that was the time when seeds of a love match between Ursula and me were sown, although it was six years before we were married. However I made a start by inviting Ursula to stay at Achnacarry, which Father had taken for the season. In the meantime I went off to Henley with the Hall crew.

Being without a car was most inconvenient so, once Henley was over, I went off to Great Portland Street, London, the centre of the second-hand car trade in those days, and bought a four-seater Aston Martin. I returned to Cambridge to collect all my gear and then headed for home. What a wonderful three years those Cambridge years had been!

Plans were made for Ursula to come up by night sleeper, arriving on the same morning as we were all setting off for Achnacarry. I met her at Kirkcaldy station and drove her back to Leslie. We arrived at breakfast time and she met all the family; it must have been quite an ordeal. She told me afterwards that Kirkcaldy was a much bigger town than she had imagined, and that she had looked up the family in Debrett to learn all the names only to find that all bar one were known by their second names.

Steam yacht on Loch Arkaig, 1930.

After the breakfast had been cleared away we prepared for the journey. Ursula and I set off before the others and according to her we agreed to meet for lunch. The route was the same as for Kintail but we did not have to go so far; we turned off just north of Spean Bridge. Achnacarry was the home of Sir Donald Cameron of Lochiel, head of the Clan Cameron. It was a large mansion set in a park and was quite imposing.

Ursula stayed for a week and, strangely, I remember little about it. I eventually put her on the night sleeper train at Fort William.

It had been agreed that I need not start work with Michael Nairn and Co. till the season was over, so I was determined to make the best of it.

Achnacarry House was situated about a mile east of Loch Arkaig and there was a large stable block between the two. Donald Cameron, the head stalker, lived there and there was accommodation for our chauffeurs and for the gillies. The gillies, headed by one called Sam, all came from Skye and were a wonderful bunch. Loch Arkaig was twelve miles long and all the land lay on the south side of the loch. There was a service road two miles up the loch after which it forked left up Glen Maley for three miles. At the end of this road there was a house occupied by David Cameron, the second stalker, who lived with his sister. The other vital part of the establishment was the steam yacht. It had quite a large cabin and could carry ten or twelve people including its crew of two. The crew were in fact the blacksmith and his mate. The yacht was not available on Thursdays as the blacksmith had to shoe ponies that day.

Father took Achnacarry for a second season and I cannot remember in which year the following occurred, probably the first year as I was there for the full season whereas in the following year I only had one week owing to limited holidays and the demands of TA camp.

The normal procedure for the stalking parties was for both parties to embark on the yacht and to steam west, picking up David Cameron on the way. When the first beat was reached the first party would be put ashore. The exact position for disembarkation was often decided by a spy of the ground from the boat. The second party steamed further west until their selected spot was chosen.

The skipper knew the probable pick-up points and he would drop anchor to suit. Very often he would spot the parties coming down and steam over; if not, the stalking party would put up a smoke signal to attract his attention. The east party would have to wait till the yacht returned and as they saw it approach they would put up their smoke signal. As the yacht neared the home jetty a long blast was blown on the steam whistle as a signal for Geordie Brown to bring the shooting brake and trailer to pick up the parties and stags. As the trips down the loch could be ten miles they lasted for some time. The skipper had welded a 3-foot long handle onto a large kettle, which was thrust into the ship's boiler and tea was served.

If the parties were very cold and wet the tea was often laced with a liberal drop of whisky. Occasionally we persuaded our Skye gillies to give us a Gaelic song.

On one occasion we spotted what looked like a van in trouble on the north side of the loch. There was a road up the north side which terminated about two miles from the end of the loch. Beyond this point there was only a track to Glendessary Lodge. The grocer's van came to the road end once a week and local residents came to meet him. On this occasion a lady had been driven by her chauffeur up to the end of the road as she wished to walk up to the lodge as her late husband had died there. They were returning down the road when they came upon the grocer's van, one wheel of which had gone through a culvert. The chauffeur thought he could drive round the van but found that it was quite easy to get down but not so easy to get up again. He had borrowed a shovel from the grocer and was trying to make a track for his car when we arrived. One of the gillies walked over to him and said, 'Man, if you are to dig your own grave you had better get started today.' We were a party of five strong men so we soon pushed the car up onto the road and sent them on their way. Manpower quite quickly sorted the grocer's van. Once out the driver opened his van and we had visions of some goodies being presented as reward for services but no, 'Anyone wish to buy anything?' he said. He nearly got thrown into the loch.

The other stalking beat was up Glen Mallie where David Cameron lived. Thursday was one of the favourite days for that beat as we had no steamer, but stalking was not confined to Thursday. David's house was about five and a half miles from the castle and we could either walk or ride up on a deer saddle. I preferred to walk. After the day's stalking Miss Cameron would not allow you to go home without a cup of tea which always included beautiful girdle scones and jam. What a delightful lady she was, so gracious and dignified and still full of fun.

Before leaving Cambridge, I had received an invitation from John deRutzen to a week's celebrations for his twenty-first birthday. This meant travelling from Achnacarry to Pembrokeshire in South Wales. I set off in my second-hand Aston Martin but by the time I got to Pitlochry it was obvious that something was wrong as the power had gone and there were some terrible noises coming from under the bonnet. A quick examination at a local garage revealed that a piston had shattered. What should I do? Do I take to the train or do I go back? Both were difficult. I took the train to Perth where I began to explore the possibilities. The plan that emerged was to take the night London train and get off at Crewe. That was something which I was very familiar with having done it many times on the way back to Shrewsbury. All went well as far as Crewe. From there it looked as if I could get a local train all the way to my destination. We left at some early hour and stopped at every station, picking up milk churns and delivering papers. Somewhere between 7.30 and 8.00 we arrived at my station and out I got. There were no buildings and only one man who was collecting the papers. I asked him if I could get a taxi. He said if I came to the village with him I could get one there. His transport was a light cart and horse, so, dumping my bag amongst the newspapers, I climbed up beside him. The journey to the village proved to be only a little over a mile. I got my hire car and was driven to what I thought was to be my destination. On arrival I rang the bell and the door was opened by a lady who was obviously not one of the family or a table-maid. I explained who I was and she said, 'Come in; I shall have to ring the big house. They have all moved up there for the week.' She rang through and said Mr John would like to speak to me.

When I spoke to John he said, 'How splendid; will you bring Mrs Cook with you?' which I of course agreed to do. It took my new found lady friend some time to shut up but the driver did not seem to mind.

Our host and hostess were Sir Frank and Lady Newnes, John's uncle and aunt who were giving the week's party. Most of the guests had not arrived but were expected before dinner. After a bite of lunch, which was very welcome as I had not fed since I left Perth, John said we must go out and shoot something for tomorrow's lunch, something to make a game pie. A gun was thrust into my hand and out we went down towards a large pond. I think the bag consisted of a curlew, a moorhen and a couple of rabbits. There were quite a lot of guests by the time we got back and we all milled around getting to know one another. John then announced in a loud voice, 'Dinner will be at 7.30,' and then came over and told us on the quiet that it would be eight o'clock but as his aunt was always half an hour late he had to make that announcement. The Trinity Hall bunch were all housed in what I think was the servants' wing. I was all for a bath so turned on the water. Out came boiling hot water but not a drop of cold. However, we donned our dinner jackets and down we went. After dinner Lady Newnes entertained the company by playing the piano and whistling, which she did very well. That set the tone for the week.

One day there was an estate garden party at which there was to be a great tug-of-war between the estate workers and farm tenants and the household. The hefty farm workers were the firm favourites. However, the household team was composed of eight rowing men and with their better co-ordination and fitness they demolished the favourites. One day we went to some races; one evening there was a ball, and on another a bonfire and fireworks. Quite a birthday party. One of the guests was John's housemaster from Eton. I discovered that he was heading for Scotland after the party and on hearing of my problem, he offered to take me with him. This meant going back to Eton for one night and then driving up in one day with two drivers. By this means I got back to Achnacarry to finish my holiday.

# CHAPTER 9

# Linoleum

On returning to Leslie I did two things. I started to work in Kirkcaldy and I joined the TA, but more about that later.

Michael Nairn & Co. was a large manufacturing company with factories covering many acres and employing some 2,000 people in Kirkcaldy. There were associated companies in the USA and Canada and subsidiaries in France and Australia.

The senior management of the company was:

Chairman and joint managing director, Sir Michael Nairn (Uncle Mike). Primary responsibility production and development.

Joint Managing Director, Sir Robert Spencer-Nairn (Father). Primary responsibility sales and finance.

Secretary, Alfred P. Peat.

Sales, Willie Black (Cousin).

Production, Michael Black (Cousin).

All the above were directors. My brother Douglas was an understudy on the sales side.

George Nairn, Sir Michael's son, who was two years younger than me, spent a year at the French plant learning the language and then started in Kirkcaldy just after me. Shortly after I started, the company took over the Greenwich Inlaid Linoleum company, one of the original companies in the trade.

The factories in Kirkcaldy were functional units. First, there was St Mary's Canvas Works. Here was woven almost all the canvas required for the production of its floorcloth and linoleum. The primary reason for weaving our own canvas was to maintain a quality that would ensure freedom from faults in subsequent operations. There were about two hundred looms, mostly 6 ft. wide but there were a few 12 ft. wide, and of course there was all the necessary finishing machinery. These works were located opposite Kirkcaldy harbour and were separated from the Floorcloth Works by Robert Hutchison's Flour Mill.

The main road passed both plants and was one of the main tram routes; there was also a steep hill known as the Path. The head office was at the top of the Path. From there on the street was called Nether Street. The original part of the Floorcloth Works were built between the Nether Street and the sea and on the side of a very steep cliff. When first built they were dubbed by the locals 'Nairn's Folly'. How wrong they were.

There were three streets running parallel to Nether Street: Commercial Street, Mid Street and finally Nairn Street. Located in this area was the Fife Linoleum Co., later taken over by us. The main oil processing and linoleum plant lay north of Nairn Street and extended well beyond the main line railway.

The oil processing was the operation which produced the smell which became so characteristic of Kirkcaldy. When I used to visit the factories as a small boy all the machines were driven by line shafts from steam engines, but by the time I started working, a large new power station had been built and conversion to electric power was nearly complete.

As far as I was concerned my training was not well organised. I was sent from plant to plant, reporting to the manager in each case.

I started at the Canvas Works where the manager was Mr Anderson. He was a rather dour chap, but tried to be helpful. In his office I found records of everything which I copied into a note book. When it came to the process it was more difficult. I managed the preparatory and finishing with not too much difficulty as they were all male operated but the weaving, that was different. First, the girls were all on piece work and second, the noise was such that you could not talk to them. The result was a rather embarrassed young man would wander round, pretending to be taking an intelligent interest in what they were doing, with some sixty or more critical female eyes on him.

All the reels of finished canvas were distributed by horse-drawn transport and when these loads were going up the Path they required an extra trace horse. This was all done by contract; the company did not own any horses.

My next move was to the Floorcloth Works. My first problem was to find my way around; part was on one side of the street and part on the other, and these were connected by overhead bridges. The main building being built on the side of the hill, there were all sorts of different levels.

Floorcloth was made by trowelling a layer of a heavily filled paint onto a piece of canvas and then hanging it in a heated stove to dry. This process was repeated until an adequate thickness was reached. A red paint back was then applied and the goods were ready for printing. All floorcloth and linoleum was hung in loops (or bights as they were known in the trade) of 45 ft. A piece was 90 ft. long. I think this applied the world over.

The printing was done on a machine. These were built in Kirkcaldy by the Melville Brodie Engineering Co. and were long (30 ft.) and quite complicated. A good printer was a really skilled man. There was still a little hand printing done for carpet squares and I enjoyed having a go at this. All the paints were made on the premises. This was quite a skilled operation in itself. I found life here more congenial as the workers were all male, the noise levels were much less and you could speak to people. Nevertheless, there was still something missing, participation. I was neither a member of a squad nor a member of management; I felt a sort of parasite.

My next move was to the block shop. It was here that all the printing blocks for both the floorcloth and the linoleum printing were made. This was a skilled job. Most of the blocks were wooden and they were normally 18 in. square or 3 ft. by 18 in. The first process was to saw draft the whole surface; this was done by machine. The pattern was then put on by transfer and finally all the unrequired area was cut away. This required great accuracy as very often patterns had six colours and all had to fit. Where there was only a very small area of pattern it was usually built up with brass pins. The men in this shop all belonged to a little craft union, known as the 'Print Block, Roller and Stamp Cutters Society'. Many years later when I was involved in union negotiations I learnt that the annual claim for wage rises had to be prolonged to finish with the final meeting in London on Cup Final day. The general secretary was a staunch Tory and a keen football follower.

From the blockshop I moved to the Linoleum Works. This was much the largest section. It was under one manager, Alex Kerss, who had a number of under-managers and foremen.

Linoleum. What is it and how is it made? By far the most important ingredient is linseed oil. It is a vegetable oil which, when exposed to the air, absorbs oxygen and forms a tough film. The other ingredients, known as fillers, are granulated cork or wood-flour and small proportions of a mineral filler, mostly whiting.

We bought linseed oil to a specification through brokers. Most of it was crushed in Hull, but some came from Rotterdam or other places. It was delivered by coastal tankers and occasionally by railway tankers. The oil that came by sea was pumped out of the ship into weighing tanks in the canvas factory and then pumped some half a mile up to the storage tanks. Although considerable quantities of oil were used for making paints it was in fact of little significance compared to that used to make linoleum.

The first process was known as oil boiling. The boilers were heated by a coal fire which could be withdrawn if necessary. The oil was stirred and air blown through it. When the required viscosity was reached the fire was withdrawn and the oil cooled.

The next process was the making of what were known as skins. This was done in a battery of sheds. Each shed was about 30 ft. high with a rack at the top and a collecting tank at the bottom. Cotton scrim was hung in a series of loops until the shed was filled. The treated oil was then poured over the scrim, the oil was recirculated and the process repeated daily for several months. When the film on the scrim reached about two inches in thickness the process was stopped and the contents removed. Many tons would come out of a shed.

After that came the conversion of the skins into linoleum cement. The skins were shredded through rollers and the shredded material was put into a large cement pot. These pots were about 5 ft. in diameter and about 7 ft. deep. They were steam heated and were fitted with a large stirrer. Resin and gum were added at this point and the cooking started. When ready it was a semi-liquid mass and it was then tipped out onto the floor. After cooling it was cut up and stored in stalls to mature.

Now I must turn to the fillers: cork, woodflour, whiting and china clay. The china clay came in bulk by boat from Cornwall, while the whiting came from the south of England. The woodflour came from local woodflour mills in bags. The real problem was the cork which came from Portugal and was a seasonal shipment. This meant that one required to have a year's storage capacity. A feature of every linoleum company was huge cork sheds. The cork was shipped in compressed bales secured by wooden slats and wire.

Cork when stripped from the trees is fairly hard and has to be treated before it becomes the nice pliable material which most of us know. This was done in Portugal. All the bottle corks were then cut out and it was the residue which came to us. When a cork boat arrived in Kirkcaldy all available transport was assembled. Cork milling was a skilled job and was originally done on stone mills, much like flour. It was milled down to 40 mesh and at that could form an explosive mixture.

The next process was the making of the final linoleum mix, which consisted of linoleum cement, cork and/or woodflour, minerals and colour pigments. This was done by shredding cement through rollers and stirring in the cork, etc. This mixture was then passed through a German mixer. This machine looked rather like a huge mincer but was very different inside. The next machine was known as a two roll and scratcher. It had two rollers, one of which was cold and the other hot. The material stuck to the cold roll, and formed a thick film on it. The scratcher was a drum covered in hackle pins. This was rotated fast and scratched the film off the cold roll leaving it in a granulated form. This material could either go direct to a calender or be stored and then it could be treated in a very large variety of ways to make different effects and designs.

The calender was a heavy machine with 30 in. diameter rolls, round one of which passed the canvas onto which the granulated material was rolled. The methods of making the many effects were too numerous and complex to describe. Once on the canvas it was hung in stoves which were heated to a little over 100°F. The time in the stove varied with the thickness of the film, from one week to three or four weeks. Linoleum was made in the following thicknesses: 1.6 mm, 2.0 mm, 3.5 mm, 4.5 mm, 6.7 mm. The linoleum mixing process was later greatly speeded up by the introduction of Banbury mixers. These were large machines driven by a 500 h.p. motor. Batches of all the materials were fed in and forced down by a hydraulic ram and then mixed together by two fancy shaped rotors. Each batch only took about four minutes to mix.

One other product must be mentioned: felt base. It consisted of a heavy paper saturated with bitumen then coated on both sides, with finally a printed pattern on one side. This was the cheapest form of floorcovering. When I started, the paper was bought in and saturated on the premises, but that did not prove satisfactory so a paper-making plant was built. This made a new process to master. Originally the raw materials were rags and waste paper, but later a wood pulping plant was added.

I think it must have been about a year after I started that George

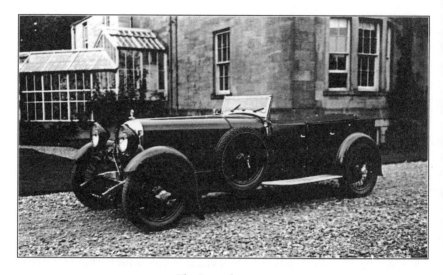

The Lagonda, 1932.

and I were sent to Greenwich to learn the processes there. We lived
in digs in Blackheath and as it was winter it was very cold. I had
acquired a beautiful ex-demonstration model 3-litre Lagonda and
one day when it was time to return from the factory one of
London's worst fogs had descended and I could not even see the
bonnet of the car. George sat on the bonnet and signalled to me and
by that method we got home.

The relaxed nature of my training had its advantages. It enabled
me to escape on Saturday mornings and go hunting. I used to work
on Saturday mornings in the summer time.

# CHAPTER 10

# The Territorial Army

Why did I join the Territorial Army?
There were two reasons. First because my father had been a member, and most of my friends were members. The second reason and the one applying to many of my friends, was because there was a very strong feeling in the country that one should do something in the way of service to King and Country. In those days the Empire still existed and many young men joined one of the Overseas services; but those that did not, joined something at home.

As the result of my certificates A and B I was granted an immediate commission. The next step was to buy the necessary uniform. I joined the 20th Armoured Car Company (Fife & Forfar Yeomanry), Royal Armoured Corps. In spite of the name we still thought that we were horsed, at least as far as our formal uniform was concerned. When on formal parades the officers wore breeches and black field boots and spurs; tunics, Sam Brown belts and cavalry-type caps completed the get-up. When in our armoured cars we wore slacks and black berets. Blue patrols and mess dress were also required for evenings in the mess.

I was posted to the Kirkcaldy Troop, commanded by Sandy McIntosh of A. H. McIntosh and Co., furniture manufacturers in Kirkcaldy. We became very close friends. Drills took place once a week in the drill hall and my job was to organise the classes from amongst those who turned up. Little or no drill was undertaken except in annual camp; instruction was confined to driving and maintenance, gunnery, and wireless.

Our home camping site was at Annsmuir at Ladybank, where there were still some wooden stalls for horses and a good wooden hut for an officers' mess. There was also a miniature range fitted with an armoured car turret and machine gun. The latter was fitted with a Morris tube which brought its calibre down to .22. We used to shoot at little model tanks drawn across the target area. This building still exists although all the rest of the area has been absorbed by Ladybank Golf Club.

I attended several annual camps at Annsmuir, but we also visited Barrie Camp at Carnoustie, Gales in Ayrshire, Dunbar in East Lothian, and Scarborough and Catterick in Yorkshire.

Mess nights (nights when we had guests to dinner and we all dressed up and the band played outside) always tended to become rather wild. At Ladybank one ploy was to challenge some guest, say from the Black Watch, to ride the bath. Each officer had a tin bath about 4 ft. in diameter and about 6 in. deep with a handle on one side. A rope was attached to this handle and the other end to the back of a car. A cushion was placed in the bath, as the friction made the bottom of the bath too hot to sit on. The competitor then sat cross-legged in the bath and his job was to stay there. The job of the driver of the car was to see that he did not. The parade ground was just an open grassy area and the driver would drive round here in a figure of eight. The bath being on the end of the rope travelled round the corners at a very much faster speed than the car. I don't remember any serious accidents, but there were many very dirty uniforms.

When we camped away we usually shared the camp with another regiment. At Gales it was the Ayrshire Yeo. There the place lived up to its name as we had a gale and in the morning the mess tent was flat with all the regimental silver inside. At Dunbar we shared with the Lothian and Border Horse. Naturally we had an exercise, the one regiment against the other. The L & BH had a young officer called Wattie McCulloch whose father was Officer Commanding Scotland. Wattie was a real joker and usually the life and soul of the party. During the exercise his car came face to face with one of ours. The two car commanders were chatting when a staff car drew up behind Wattie's car. At the back of our cars there were two tool boxes, one on either side. Wattie saw his father descend from the staff car and walk up to the back of his car. Great was his alarm when his father started to open one of the boxes, as he knew that they were full of beer bottles. Father quietly shut the lid and nothing more was heard of it. I wonder what passed between father and son afterwards.

On another occasion we were at Annsmuir when an exercise was arranged with the RAF. They said they wanted some practice at identifying armoured vehicles on the road. An area was agreed and we proceeded there. Some quite small planes came over and obviously saw us. We thought that was that, but no. They returned and proceeded to shower us with masses of small paper bags full of flour. A direct hit with one of these was very obvious.

One summer Sandy McIntosh suggested that the Kirkcaldy Troop should have a weekend exercise, and camp somewhere for one night. We had only one armoured car but we managed to borrow another one so our force comprised two cars and a 15 cwt. truck. This was important as it carried all the stores and a fitter in case of breakdown. We camped the Saturday night at Newtonmore and planned to return by Fort William and Glencoe. We arrived at Ballachulish ferry and proceeded to load the first car. As the little boat set off we noticed that the water was almost lapping the sides. Thank God it got across safely: the loss of an armoured car at sea would have been the subject for a court martial. We had never noticed the little notice on the ferry which said 'Maximum load 3 tons'. The car weighed over 5 tons. I am afraid the second car had to drive all the way round by Kinlochleven.

The year before I joined, a little incident occurred at Barry Camp which I think is worth recording. Fergus McIntyre had just joined and there was to be an inspection by some senior officer. Now, Fergus was not a natural soldier and he had not yet become proficient either in drill or in any technical subject so the CO decided that Fergus would be excused the parade and would be sent away into the sand dunes with a machine gun and an instructor. In those days some of the senior officers brought horses with them and the General suggested that he would like to have a ride. Two horses were produced and off went the CO and the General. As luck would have it, they rounded a sand dune and there was Fergus and his instructor having a nice chat.

'And what are you doing here, young man?' said the General.

'Hiding from you, Sir,' was the reply.

The General rode on.

As the RR armoured cars with their Vickers machine guns were a fairly new issue to us, I was asked if I would go on a two week gunnery course at Lulworth, with the object of becoming the regimental gunnery officer. As it was to be in mid-summer I thought it would be rather fun so I agreed to go. I did not have to take my black field boots, but I did have to take my blue patrols and mess dress for dinner.

On arrival I was allotted a room in a wooden hut and a soldier servant. There were only one or two other officers in the hut and the servant looked after us all. There was a bath at the end of the hut with its own little boiler outside. If you wished a bath you told your servant and he stoked up the boiler. The course was a mixed one with regular officers as well as TA ones. The instructors were all NCOs, and very good they were. When I left that course I knew the name and function of every piece of a Vickers machine gun.

We young officers found dinner in the mess rather a bore. As the Duke of Gloucester was there; we were not allowed to leave the table until he did and he loved to linger and enjoy his port.

There was one sad thing happened while I was there. A regiment were on the ranges and they had a fatal accident, one of their soldiers being shot and killed. On the brighter side, a young New Zealander from Cambridge called Mallory whom I knew was playing in a hard court tennis tournament in Bournemouth which was quite near. He asked me to go along in the evening and said he would get me in for free. On arrival I found that this meant me taking a line. Fortunately, I was allotted the service line which meant I could watch the rest of the game. The famous Fred Perry was playing.

Two years later I was sent on a driving and maintenance course at Bovington. There I was taught all about how a Silver Ghost Rolls Royce worked. After this I felt that I was well trained; the only technical course I had not been on was a wireless course.

Our Regimental Colonel at this time was Colonel Carnegie. He happened to be a Gentleman at Arms and was to be on duty at a levée to be held by King George V at St James' Palace. As he was on duty, Jo (the Colonel) was anxious to have a member of the Regiment presented. Whoever was presented would have to parade in full dress uniform. As this was peculiar to the regiment it could not be hired, and to buy it was very expensive. I was in a very favourable position as Father had a uniform. His tunic and trousers were no use as he was smaller than me, but my mess dress trousers were the same so all I had to get was a scarlet tunic with all its silver braid. Father's silver helmet and plume, his bandolier, his waist belt, sword frog and sword were all available for me. The helmet was too big but I did not have to wear it, only carry it. So after debate it was decided that I should be the one to go.

When the day came I took all my tin boxes to the Cavalry Club where I knew these things would be understood and where I could get a valet to ensure I was properly dressed.

I took a taxi to St James' Palace and presented my official card. There were not a great number on parade, but they included all ranks, from Generals down to the small-fry like me. It was a wonderful sight, every one in full dress, with the passages and staircase lined with guardsmen interspersed with Gentlemen. We were formed into a sort of queue in order of seniority with me at the tail end. With a thick tunic buttoned up to the neck and carrying a helmet, it became hot and tiring. I knew that Jo was to be on duty standing directly behind the throne, so I was determined not to catch his eye as I knew he would wink at me or something worse. When my turn came and my name was announced I marched in the regulation number of paces, halted, turned right, made my bow from the neck only, then left turned and marched out. As far as I could see the King was fast asleep. I made my way to the Gentlemen's Mess where I had arranged to meet Jo.

As I was one of the last through, all the Gentlemen were leaving their posts and heading for the mess, very exhausted. I kept hearing, as each one entered, a husky voice call out, 'A glass of port.' After our refreshment we all dispersed to get changed before lunch. It was quite a memorable occasion.

In 1931 my cousin Willie Black got married and he asked me to be his best man. He married Nancy Grimond of St Andrews and they went to live at Teasses. The next year my brother Douglas got married and I got the same job again. He married Elizabeth Henderson, sister of Hearty Henderson whom he had known at Cambridge. They went to live at Barham where we had spent our early life. At home life went on. In the winter I hunted most Saturdays and in the summer played some tennis and the occasional game of golf. All this time I had kept in touch with Ursula by the odd letter and she came as my guest to the dinner party after Douglas's wedding which was in London.

In 1931 father returned to Achnacarry, but I only had one week there owing to the demands of TA camp.

I don't know what the excuse was but at the end of October I left for Canada. I sailed in the *Empress of Britain*, the CPR's newest liner. We sailed for Quebec and I was able to enjoy that wonderful sight of the Citadel as we sailed up the St Lawrence. I stayed with the Prices whose family included Enid who had stayed with us for eighteen months some four years earlier. They were a large family of I think eight, all of whom were at home and although it was a short stay it was great fun. I then moved on to Montreal where I met Archie Baillie, Chairman and Managing Director of the

Dominion Oilcloth and Linoleum Company. I also met Frank McGill, and the Roberton brothers, Ken and Gordie. The latter showed me round the works and entertained me in his home. This was the first of quite a number of visits.

I then moved on to New York, all of this by train as there were no aeroplanes. Al Hawkes, the Chairman of Congoleum-Nairn, had arranged for me to stay in the Union Club from where I was picked up by a chauffeur driven car and driven to Karney, going through the Hudson River tunnel. After a brief meeting with Al I was handed over to a young man whose job was to show me something of the plants and to entertain me in the evenings. These were the days of prohibition and I was informed that my young guide's father was a member of Tamany Hall, a body which seemed to have great influence, especially with the police. I was given a card and told that if I was in a speakeasy and it was raided by the police I should go quietly and then show my card to them in the police van and that I would then be let free. I never had to use it.

It so happened that I was in New York on the night of the presidential election and was being entertained in a restaurant in Times Square. Roosevelt was standing against President Hoover on the ticket of the removal of prohibition. There was drink served but all the bottles were kept well out of sight. We watched the results coming in on the lights across the Square and as Roosevelt surged further and further ahead the bottles became more and more obvious. I visited one or two private homes, all of whom had their private boot-legger and plenty of drink. I returned home by a White Star Liner.

In 1932 Father took stalking at Glencanisp. Glencanisp was just a few miles east of Lochinver and the ground stretched almost to Inchnadamph. Sometimes we motored round there and stalked home. There were a number of ponies running on the place which had not been handled for years and were for all intents and purposes wild. There were a number of areas into which we could not take the ponies owing to the nature of the ground. As these areas were usually boggy and flat and therefore difficult for dragging, the gillies used to cut the stag into three pieces: the head and neck, the forequarters and the hind quarters, and carry it out. They had however a very curious habit. They took off their jackets and turned them inside out before picking up their loads; by this means, the bloodstains were all on the inside and on returning home they could reverse their jackets and look respectable again. For whose benefit this was done, I never discovered.

Father took it again for 1933 and when I was up for my short week he and Mother went off to inspect Struy with a view to buying it. Left in the house were myself, Sheila, one of the Price girls from Canada aged about twenty and Aunt Helen, one of Mother's spinster sisters. Aunt Helen could have been only in her mid to late fifties but we thought she was aged. She thought that she ought to chaperon us and would not go to bed until we did. I am afraid we enjoyed pulling her leg. Changed days!

# CHAPTER 11

# Australia and New Zealand

I think that it was in the early autumn of 1933 that I first heard whispers about Uncle Mike making a trip to Australia, accompanied by Aunt Mildred, George, and Barbara, their youngest daughter. I was of course envious of such a wonderful trip, but great was my joy when it was suggested that I should go too to keep George company. The plan was that we should sail in the P & O liner *Strathnaver* in January 1934 and that we should return via New Zealand and the USA by the end of April.

My mother hated the long cold winters, as Father hunted and she had nothing to do. When she heard about this trip she thought it would be fun to join in as far as Egypt and make a trip up the Nile. Of course she did not wish to go alone so she decided to take her maid and her eldest daughter, my sister Matilda, then twenty. The next problem was who would keep Matilda company, and this was solved by asking Ursula to join the party.

There followed a period of great activity. It would be hot in Australia, and of course we would have to sail through the tropics. All this meant that we would require all sorts of light-weight clothes, including white cotton jackets for evening wear on board. How did you carry all these clothes? There was no problem about how much luggage you took, as there were always plenty of porters to hump it about for you. I bought myself what was called a cabin trunk and a huge heavy expanding suitcase. The trunk was about 18 inches square and a little over 3 feet high. It stood on one end and the other end was domed so you could not stand it upside down. It had hinges down the back and opened down the centre. On one side, when open, it provided hanging space on one side and drawers on the other side.

Eventually the great day came and what a party we were, five in the Australian party and four in the Egyptian party. I was, of course, delighted that Ursula was with us as I was becoming rather fond of her. Our first stop was Gibraltar. Here we all went ashore, explored the Rock and had lunch in a hotel before returning to our ship. There were all sorts of sporting activities available on deck, including a form of miniature tennis played with a solid racquet rather like an oversized ping-pong bat, then there were deck quoits and bull, but no ping-pong. On board there was a certain Mr Smith, aged about fifty, who appointed himself unofficial sports director. He was upset by the lack of ping-pong and asked the purser if space could be made on board if he bought a table at Marseilles, our next port of call. The purser said that would be quite in order. I don't think many of us went ashore at Marseilles but Mr Smith did and returned followed by a string of porters carrying the two halves of a table, its trestle, and boxes of equipment. It was put in place and Mr Smith proceeded to run tournaments.

I think our next port of call was Alexandria where the Egyptian party disembarked. Having passed through the Suez Canal we made a brief stop at Port Sudan. I had never been in the Middle East and was fascinated just to watch the scene and the hordes of humanity that accompanied every activity. We made another brief stop at Aden before sailing on to Bombay.

We had a full day here so we all went ashore. Aunt Mildred and Barbara stayed at a large hotel from which they could make short forays to the immediate shops, but not so the three men. Uncle Mike had been supplied with a list of customers at every port of call. It was decided that we should visit one so we hired a taxi and off we set. Further and further down town we went until we arrived in a fairly narrow street with open fronted little shops and plenty of holy cows. Finally we came to rest in front of one of these little shops. Our driver explained that we wished to see the boss and he was produced. He could speak very, very little English so with the help of our driver we tried to explain our mission. Eventually he shot inside and returned with a file of invoices, all from Barry Ostler and Shepherd, our main rival in Kirkcaldy. The shop was too small and over-full of everything imaginable to get into, so all our discussions took place in the crowded street amongst the chickens and cows and an ever increasing crowd of locals. So much for our goodwill mission.

We piled into our taxi and were delighted to leave the smells behind, and sailed that night for Colombo where we made only a brief stop. From here we set off on the long leg to Fremantle; this took several days during which we saw no other ships. We made a very brief stop off some islands where stores were off-loaded into small boats.

On the morning that we were due to dock at Fremantle we awoke to find all the lounges bare of everything. On enquiring the reason we were informed that the public were allowed on board and that any loose thing left about would disappear in seconds.

We were met by Tomlinson, our Western Australian agent, and his son John who must have been about twenty at that time. John became a great friend and Ursula and I stayed with Debbie and him on several future occasions. We were driven in two cars to Perth where we alighted at the Promenade Hotel. This was a beautiful old wooden colonial building with verandas and balconies, and was run by a family whom everyone knew in Western Australia. After a leisurely lunch we, the males, visited our main customers. Perth was really quite a small place in those days.

We sailed on to Melbourne where we were met by Scott Melville, our chief Australian salesman. Scott lived in Melbourne but had originally come out from Kirkcaldy. Outwardly he appeared a dour man but he really had a nice sense of humour and he was very much respected in the trade. We paid many visits to customers here before sailing on for Sydney. It was at about this point that Mr Smith approached the purser, full of hope of receiving full compensation for the cost of the ping-pong table and equipment. Great was his disappointment when he was told by the purser that he had no authority to purchase other than expendable stores and that ping-pong tables could not be classed as such. It was suggested to him that on his return to the UK he should make his claim at the P & O office in London. This was not good enough for Mr Smith so he left the ship with his table as part of his luggage. I thought to myself, Good on 'in. Yes, we had a number of Aussies on board who had taught us a little Australian.

We sailed through the Heads, the entrance to Sydney Harbour, quite early in the morning and everybody was on deck to watch us sail under the famous Sydney Harbour Bridge and dock. The bridge was still quite new and large crowds had assembled on the bridge to watch us sail underneath.

We were met by Mr Phillips, Chairman of Michael Nairn (Australia) Ltd, and taken to the Australia Hotel in Castlereigh Street. This was *the* hotel in Sydney at that time and was quite a sizeable building. It was being extended to give it a second entrance in Martin Place. My room looked over the work site and Oh! the noise! That first day was spent settling in and exploring the immediate area of the hotel. One of our immediate discoveries was that you had to be in the dining room by 6.00 p.m. if you wished to get any dinner.

The ladies were entertained by various friends, all of whom had been well warned of our arrival, while the men were taken out to the factory at Auburn, which was on the way to Paramatta, several miles to the north-west of the city. A mile or so before turning off the main road to the factory we passed through an area of large paddocks with high stockade fencing, well filled with animals. The air was full of a strong pungent odour which we soon discovered came from a huge slaughter house. On arrival at the factory we met John Melville, son of Scott, in charge of sales, Madrell in charge of production and the accountant, Hugh Doran. The factory had been built by Jimmy Laing, an architect, and an engineer, both from Kirkcaldy, but who had returned to Scotland. George and I spent one or two days at the factory while Uncle Mike had meetings with Mr Phillips, the manager of the Bank of New South Wales and other important people. I remember George and me being photographed sitting on top of a load of linoleum on a lorry about to leave the factory.

I do not remember much about any social life in Sydney but we were taken on a long drive through the Blue Mountains and on to Canberra where we stayed in the only hotel for one or two nights. There was no large lake in those days and it was all terribly new. At one time we young ones, including Barbara, stayed with some friends of George and Barbara's at Yass. We were taken to the Yass Picnic Races and to a Race Ball afterwards. The ball was held in a public hall in the town and Oh, was it hot! We men were all dressed up in white ties and boiled shirts. Most of the local men kept popping out to change their collars which had collapsed but we were quite unprepared for this.

During our stay in Sydney we made many visits to customers and trips by ferry to the zoo and other places of interest. It was all immensely interesting and, of course, great fun.

We sailed on a Thursday for a five-day trip across the Timor Sea to Wellington, New Zealand. We were met on arrival by Gabriel Young, our New Zealand agent. He was a typical Scot, with large bushy eyebrows. He had spent several years in Eastern Canada before taking over in New Zealand.

I think we had about two weeks available before we had to sail from Auckland for the USA. George and I decided that we would see as much as we could in the time available and arranged to go off on our own and meet up again in Auckland in time to catch the boat. We took the overnight ferry to Christchurch where we hired a car. I had arranged to visit Harold Elworthy and his family at Timaru, but we thought we had time just to drive up to Mt. Cook Hotel for a night. All the roads were just gravel and the cars old so progress was slow. We got there however and who should we meet but a man who had been on the *Strathnaver*. He said he had been hunting thar and chamois and would we like to go out with him next day. We had a wonderful day climbing over glaciers and rocks and I managed to shoot a thar and I think George got a chamois. Both these animals were imported as were all other game. The thar came from the Himalayas and the chamois from Switzerland. The head of that thar adorned the walls at Balgeddie for many years, but we had to get rid of it when we moved to West Hall.

After this unexpected but most enjoyable interlude, we moved on to Timaru. Harold was of course there and he had some rather attractive sisters, one of whom persuaded me to go hunting with the harriers and of course herself. The country was almost all wire and the horses had all been trained to jump it, a novel experience for me. We returned to Christchurch, got rid of our car and took the night ferry back to Wellington. Earlier we had arranged through Gabriel to hire a car which we could leave at Auckland and that he would arrange for it to be returned to Wellington.

We planned to go first to Nelson, where there had been a terrific earthquake about two years before. As we were passing through Hamilton there was an earth tremor and several chimney pots arrived in the street. Nelson had been a typical seaside town with a sea wall, a road and a row of water front hotels and houses. When we got there there was only one hotel which was partially habitable, and the sea was about half a mile away. The whole of the sea bed had risen up and there was a sort of desert area where the sea used to be. I wonder what it all looks like today, sixty years on.

From Nelson we drove to the south end of Lake Taupo where we were told there was a fishing station and very good trout fishing. On arrival we found one largish wooden building and a number of what looked like over sized dog kennels. On enquiry we were informed that we could hire one of the dog kennels, which was little bigger than a railway sleeper compartment and had two bunks one above the other. We also learnt that a certain Mr Frost would be available to take us fishing next day and provide all the necessary tackle. It was raining hard, so after a short walk we fed at six o'clock and spent the evening chatting to the locals. Next day it was still raining but Mr Frost took us out in a boat and we slogged away all day and never caught a thing. Lake Taupo is many miles long and wide so we only saw a tiny corner of it. That evening after supper we were again chatting with some locals when Frost came in.

'The fishing doesn't seem too good, does it? What about going for a pig hunt tomorrow?'

After discussing this project for some time it was decided that it was on.

The plan was that after an early breakfast we should take our car and drive down a gravel track until we came to a stream; there we should wait until a Maori called Dean Warratine arrived with his dogs. After a short wait he appeared riding bareback on a pony with two rather mongrel looking dogs. He rode through the stream, dismounted and set the pony free. 'He will go home,' he said.

Fortunately our car was an open four-seater with a hood so we all piled in and returned to base where we found Frost waiting. He had an old First World War rifle and some ammo. It was again raining heavily; however we all climbed back in and off we set up the road.

After a few miles through the forest, Dean suddenly said, 'Stop,' so we drew into the side. It was still wet but not cold. George tossed up as to who should be the rifleman and George won. The plan was that we should proceed into the forest in single file with Dean leading with his dogs. We set off in silence with the dogs roaming widely. After some considerable time, Dean froze and whispered, 'Pig!' Then we heard the dogs giving tongue.

We advanced slowly in the direction of the sound, and after a few minutes came upon them with a large black boar at bay facing the dogs and with its back to a high bank. The dogs were not actually in contact with the pig but were barking at it, one on either side.

The end of a succesful pig hunt. Lake Taupo, New Zeland 1934.

We approached to within twenty yards or so and George was told to shoot it. Steadying himself against a tree he fired, a perfect shot. The brute was gralloched and hung up on a tree where the dogs could not reach it.

We then stood around chatting and Frost, lighting a cigarette, said, 'I tell you what we will do next time; we will show you the way it used to be done before firearms came in. It goes like this: you try and get the dogs into the hold position, one on either side and gripping the pig by its throat. The hunter then, with his knife between his teeth, creeps up behind the pig, seizes it by a hind leg and throws it over onto its back, then, taking his knife from his mouth he cuts its throat.'

Fortunately it was not suggested that I should be the one to do this, but Frost. Off we went again and after some time Dean stopped again; we heard the dogs and we started to follow them. I was carrying the rifle this time. This time it took a little longer before we came up with our quarry as there was no convenient place for the pig to go to bay, so he kept moving with the dogs attacking him from both sides. Eventually they got a hold of him, one on either side, and Frost started, but almost immediately the pig broke free and started darting at each one of us in turn, though it was always turned by the dogs before it reached us. We in our turn kept darting behind trees. This continued for a few minutes until the dogs got a hold of it again. It appeared that the pig was tiring and Frost started to creep in again. He was just about to seize it when it broke free again and swishing round charged straight at him.

Now, these pigs have sharp tusks which can cause a serious wound, so all sorts of visions went through my mind. Frost slipped and as he fell the pig shot through underneath him, with the dogs after it. They caught it again and I shot it before any further damage was done. Frost was lucky; the pig's tusk had torn a large hole in his trouser leg but missed his leg.

After the gralloch and a brief rest we started our return journey to the car, picking up the first one on the way. We ate our lunch at the car and returned to camp, very wet but triumphant.

Tisdalls of Auckland set up these two heads for us and shipped them home. Mine had the same fate as the thar's.

Dean was a fine singer and sang at a Maori concert in front of the Duke and Duchess of York, later King George VI and Queen Elizabeth. Some record company got hold of him and recorded all his songs but never paid him a penny.

From Taupo we moved to Wairacki to explore the geyser valley. What an extraordinary place, with pools of almost boiling water bubbling up and running down the hill and only a few yards away a stream of beautiful clear cold water. We were invited up to someone's house where all the domestic water, hot and cold, was piped direct from outside. They had a small swimming pool, but it was much too hot for me; after a few strokes you were quite exhausted. The geyser valley is no more; it has all been harnessed for a thermal power station.

Time was getting short so we made only a short stop at Rotarua and so to Auckland. On the way I called on Jack Robertson, an ex-Trinity Hall man, and in Auckland I met Peter Nathan of Nathan's Store who had coxed one of the boats I had rowed in. During the war he was very kind and sent Ursula several food parcels.

Our party was all together again now when we received a cable from Kirkcaldy to tell us that there had been an explosion in the factory and that Michael Black, Douglas my brother and Kerss the factory manager were all in hospital. This made it rather urgent that at least some of us should get home as soon as possible. As I was the odd one out I was the obvious one, so I went to Thos. Cook's to explore the possibilities. The first boat was the *Monterey*, a United States liner, the one we were already booked on. Cook's promised to cable their Los Angeles office to see what they could do for me from there on. As we went on board, who should follow us but Mr Smith and, what's more, he still had his ping-pong table with him, but sport on board was so fully organised that he was out of a job. All life on board was in fact much too organised and with a telephone in every cabin you got no peace.

We had a very pleasant stop at Honolulu and in due time we arrived at Los Angeles. Cook's representative met me and told me that I could get on a flight to Newark the following morning if I was prepared to go. I had only once been up in an aeroplane before and thought it would be rather exciting so I agreed. The others were to go by train to New York and then make a visit to Congoleum-Nairn at Kearney. Next morning I took leave of our party, put all my heavy luggage in their care and took a taxi to the airport. I was met by my Cook's friend who told me that they had cabled their New York office asking them to book me onto the first available liner sailing for the UK.

Before boarding the aircraft we were weighed with our luggage. As I was waiting for this to happen I was approached by a man with two large cases who asked me if my little case was all my luggage to which I replied, 'Yes.'

'Could you take one of mine, as otherwise, being a heavy man myself, I shall be well over weight and charged a lot extra.'

I obliged.

Our plane was quite small, carrying about twelve passengers. It was a three-motor Ford of the Lindburgh Line. After take-off we seemed to go round and round over the city as we climbed and then we moved away to land almost immediately. The place looked like a desert and I wondered what was happening when out from behind a huge rock drove a petrol tanker. I was told that we required a full load of gas for our next leg to New Mexico City. I don't remember all the places we stopped at but I do remember Kansas City. We got our meals during these stops. We arrived at Newark early in the morning after a total journey time of about twenty-two hours.

I got a taxi to the station and took the train to New York, which did not have an airport at that time. I discovered that all Cook's had been able to get me was an inside cabin on the *Mauretania* and a pretty miserable cabin it was, hot and airless. And so a memorable trip drew to a close but I wished that it had had a happier ending.

# CHAPTER 12

# Home again. I get engaged

O n returning home, I learnt the sad news that Alex Kerss had died and of course his funeral had been some weeks ago. I went to see his widow and two teen-aged children: what a sad moment. Michael Black, who had not been so badly burnt, was back at work. As far as I can remember, Douglas was out of hospital but not at work and he was badly scarred about the face and hands.

Tommy Robb, a tiny man of about 5 feet 2 inches, was appointed factory manager in place of Alex. Tom had been in charge of all the wage rates and bonus schemes and knew the administration side very well, but he was no technician. David Finlay, a practical man, was appointed as his deputy and a very good team they made. My job was to relieve Michael of his overload. I do not remember how long it was before Uncle Mike and his party returned.

Before going on our trip I had decided to trade in my Lagonda as I thought it would be a waste sitting there doing nothing for four months. That at least was what I said publicly, but in truth I really wanted an excuse to order a new car. I ordered what was to be my dream car, a 3-litre Bentley. Bentleys had quite recently been taken over by Rolls Royce and this was to be one of the first of the new models. Few of the more expensive cars had standard bodies in those days and my car was to be fitted with a drop head coupé body made by Thrup & Maberley. When open it had fitted tonneau covers over the hood and another for the rear and passenger's seats. After all that build-up I cannot remember taking delivery of it, but it proved a great favourite. It was laid up during the war, but we had a wonderful Norwegian trip in it afterwards. Unfortunately it was not a good family car so when we had four children I sold it with over 100,000 miles on the clock and replaced it with a standard four-door saloon Bentley.

In 1932 I had my first ride in the Fife point-to-point on an old horse of father's called Painter. He was slow and had a hard mouth but was a safe jumper. I think we got round. The next year, Douglas having left home, I got the ride on Hewilldo. He was a good horse and half brother to Hessle Lad on whom Charles Herdman had won for Father. I had a great tussle with Ronnie Hutchison, with some bumping and boring at some of the flags. This gave me a real love of the sport and I determined to have my own horse just as soon as possible. I had, of course, been away during the 1934 season but started looking for a horse on my return. I heard of one through John Inglis which was owned by a farmer called Young at Blink-bonny Farm, Kelso, so off I went to have a look. I rode him and liked him so bought him. His name was Bandmaster. On getting him home I started riding him in the early mornings and, after my New Zealand experience, started to teach him to jump wire. He got quite good but I never really used it in the hunting field as too many of the bare wire fences had barbed top wires.

Some time about the end of 1933 Father got possession of Struy and it now became a race against time to get it ready and furnished in time for the 1934 season. The two essential things which my parents wished installed were electric light and central heating. The house had to be wired and an oil engine and generator put in place, and in addition a boiler house built and all the piping run. Moncur of Edinburgh did the heating and Martins of Kirkcaldy the electrics. Finally everything was ready.

In July the factory closed for the annual holiday and I went to TA camp, but don't remember where it was held. How bad one's memory has become; somehow both Ursula and I arrived at Struy but neither of us can remember how we got there or how we left.

I know I must have enjoyed it however as things were definitely warming up between us.

Father bought Struy from Colonel Cooper, who in turn had bought it from Lovat Estates in 1920. It was sold by the present Lord Lovat's father, which was something much regretted by Sheni (the present Lord Lovat).

The staff at Struy when Father took possession, all of whom remained, were as follows:

Peter McDonald, farm and estate manager, lived in the farm house in the village. Peter must have been in his late fifties or early sixties. He had been head stalker at Braulin before moving down to Struy. He was a short thick man with a large bald head and the palest of blue eyes. He had a delightful wife and three children. His elder son was away from home and working in a bank, and his daughter was married. His younger son Charlie was just like his father in build but was unfortunately a little mentally unstable

Donnie McGillivary was the head stalker. He was aged about twenty-eight and lived with his mother at Dumnaglass. He was a big man with the largest hands I have ever seen. He was the most likeable character and became a great favourite with us all. He had started at Struy as a boy and stayed with us until he died.

Kennie Fraser was aged about forty. He was second stalker and lived at Culligran. John McCall, shepherd and third stalker lived in the village as did the full time gardener called Brookman.

Struy proved to be an enormous joy to my father and mother for the rest of their lives, and has continued to be so to us, our family and to many friends. Much more of it will be heard as my story continues.

Back at Leslie, Father had bought a two-horse motor horse-box which made life much easier so long as no more than two horses were required. I was much enjoying Bandmaster, but at times he was quite a handful. By this time Matilda had also started hunting and father had bought a huge black animal to carry her side-saddle; it was a dull old thing but a safe conveyance.

I remember one occasion around Christmas when Father, Matilda and I all wished to go out. The meet was to be at Eden-wood so it was decided that I would hack on with Wattie on Father's horse, leading Black Sands for Matilda. Late on Friday evening a message came from the stables that Wattie was prostrate with flu. There was only one solution: I should have to take over. Fortunately, Bell and Geordie were available to feed and get the horses ready. I had to leave soon after 8.30 with about a ten mile hack ahead of me with my three horses. We were there on time, hunted all day and then it was my job to hack them home again. When we arrived back at the stables but there was no sign of life at all. I popped the horses into their boxes and had a look round, to find that the other two had also retired to bed. Off came my jacket and I set to work. By the time I had got them unsaddled, watered, fed, roughly rubbed down and rugged up I was late for dinner. I am afraid I did not clean the saddlery that night, but I did check the horses before going to bed. I slept well. Next morning Wattie came out and helped with the feeding and mucking out. I doubt if I made the Kirk that day as there were other horses to be cared for.

Every year the Fife Hunt Ball was held in the County Buildings in Cupar early in January. A large party always went from Leslie House. There would be Pa and Ma and a couple to keep them company and a number of us young ones. The older ones were driven there, and of course home again, by Bell, but we drove ourselves in the shooting brake which could carry up to ten. The driver dropped his passengers at the door and then went off to park the car. There was no anti-freeze so you rugged the car up well if it looked like frost. If it was hard frost you darted out about every hour, started up the car, gave it a run up and then went back to the ball. On returning home you again dropped your passengers and drove the car up to the garage. There were two reasons for this: it might freeze, and Father did not like cars left outside the house. Was it really worth it?

In March each year the Hunter Improvement Society held their annual stallion show at Islington. Father was a council member and on one or two occasions I was roped in to help as a steward. In any case it was a good excuse to get down to London and possibly see Ursula. In 1935 a theatre party was organised and she was invited. She had just had her tonsils out and my mother thought it would be good for her to come away for a few days so she returned home with us. Within days we were engaged and I obtained provisional approval from my future father-in-law by telephone. I returned to Sevenoaks with Ursula to obtain official approval. By this time I knew Mr Devitt quite well and he knew me. The engagement was announced on 29 March, the day of the Linlithgow and Stirlingshire point-to-point which we attended but did not have a horse entered. That Hunt has ceased to exist owing to industrial development.

Once the Fife point-to-point was over the serious matter of organising a wedding began. Fortunately the bulk of this landed on the Devitt family and our main problem was fixing a date. We did not want too long an engagement as we had known each other for six years, but these things did take time. For some reason or other it could not be before August and Father said his earliest date after that would be after 20 October, the end of the stalking season, so it was fixed for 25 October.

My main problem was finding somewhere for us to live. We heard that Tommy and Katherine Elmhurst had bought Lahill at Upper Largo from the Miss Rintouls but wished to let it as Tommy had just been appointed Air Attaché in Turkey. Ursula tells me that I motored south in my Bentley and that we visited K and Tommy at some RAF base; anyway we came to terms. K was my cousin, being a sister of Willie and Michael Black. My mother then came in and helped with the furnishing and the finding of staff, who would have to be *in situ* on our return from honeymoon.

It was suggested that Robert Redpath, who had been footman at Leslie for some time and was looking for promotion, should come to us as butler and as we knew each other well I thought that it was a splendid idea. Mother found us a cook called Ella who had flaming red hair and proved a great success. She also found Chrissie Smith as housemaid. Fat Chrissie stayed with us until she got married to Bob Gordon, one of the Leslie garden staff. We kept in touch with them until they both died. The house was partially furnished and as my parents had given us a specially built bedroom suite we were not too badly off.

That summer Father took us and Matilda to Ascot, the only time I have ever been. We all stayed in London at the favourite Brown's Hotel. I had my girl by then so the other girls and their dresses were not of too much interest to me.

St George's, Hanover Square was selected by Ursula for the wedding as she thought Sevenoaks would be too difficult for all the Scottish contingent to get to. For some peculiar reason I had to deposit a suitcase there for some weeks before the wedding to establish my residency in the parish. How stupid can you get? Great lists of guests were prepared and invitations printed. I got the job of sending them out to our relations, but I am sure I got help from my mother. It did not seem long before the presents started coming in and they all had to be listed and thanked for. Then all of a sudden it was July and off I had to go to camp. All this time I was trying to do my job in the factory in Kirkcaldy.

In September I shot down to London for Peter Devitt's wedding to Stephanie Swan, a very good excuse to see Ursula again. Somewhere along the line I had arranged with brother Frank to be my best man and a ring was bought. I managed to fit in a few days stalking at Struy and then the great trek to Brown's Hotel started.

We arrived off the night sleeper to find all our accommodation in order except that there was no room for the bridegroom, and the hotel was full. A small storm blew up but the management assured me that they would fix it so off I went for the day. On returning to the hotel I found that my room was to be the blocked off end of one of the passages, a screen having been used for this purpose. It proved adequate but was devoid of any ventilation. I don't remember any form of stag party, but I do remember that Frank and I left the ring at Collingwood the Jewellers in Conduit Street to be picked up on the way to the church on the wedding day.

# CHAPTER 13

# Marriage

Friday 25 October was a dry day. I don't remember how I spent the morning nor where I had lunch but I do remember walking up Conduit Street with Frank to collect the ring from Collingwood on the way to the church.

To describe the wedding I cannot do better than quote a local newspaper.

Wedding between M. Alastair Spencer-Nairn and Miss Ursula H. Devitt.

The bride, tall and golden haired, chose a gown which fell into beautiful lines in the skirt, the neck was simply draped and a row of minute brocade-covered buttons ran down the back. Her voluminous veil of white tulle was held by a coronet of orange blossom. The flowers she carried were arum lilies and mimosa. Two little girls in peach taffeta picture frocks with wreaths of golden leaves in their hair, carrying tiny gilt baskets of bronze flowers, led the retinue. They were Donetta Woollcombe, a cousin of the bride, and Margaret Spencer-Nairn. There followed Sheila, twin sister of the bride, two other sisters of the bridegroom, Matilda and Clare, then Diana Harrison, Monica Grayson and Patricia McGrath. Their deep red velvet dresses had effectively draped skirts and heavy gold belts of Italian design. They had gold leaf head dresses and wore brooches that were a present of the bridegroom.

Our Wedding.

The ceremony was performed by the Bishop of Buckingham, assisted by the Rev. P. Woollcombe, uncle of the bride, and the Rev. Montgomery Campbell, vicar of St George's. The reception was held at Sunderland House, Curzon Street, and there were some five hundred guests.

As far as the service was concerned, I think it was a little too long, but having three clergymen all of whom had to play a part, I suppose that was inevitable. The bishop gave us a very long pep talk, none of which I can remember, but it must have been effective as we are still together after fifty-nine years.

On leaving the Church we had the usual photographs, and another lot were taken at Sunderland House. The reception party was lined up and the guests poured in. 'I am Ursula's aunt, I am Uncle Stanley,' went on until we were completely confused. Eventually we were presented with glasses of champagne and the toasts followed. Neither of us can remember who proposed the health but he must have been from the Devitt camp.

Eventually the time came for us to change and I was conducted up a back stair where I saw two men sitting gazing out of the window, 'What are these blokes doing?' I asked, to be informed that they had been there in the morning when Frank had brought my suitcase along. When asked, they said that they were detectives watching a house on the other side of the street.

Once changed we left for the Dorchester where we had planned to stay the night. After another change into a dinner jacket we walked to Dover Street where we dined in a favourite little restaurant of mine called Maison Basque. Here you could get, when in season, the most delicious roast woodcock.

We had to be up early next morning to get to London Docks to board an Orient liner for Majorca. At the docks we were met by Mr Devitt who must have been up early to see us off.

We had a beautiful cabin, which was not surprising as Ursula's grandfather had been one of the founders of the Orient line. We had calm conditions all the way and even Ursula did not feel seasick. When in our cabin we could hear a male voice in the next cabin which sounded as if he was reading to someone. Quite soon we saw our neighbours emerge from their cabin; they were the other young couple who we thought must be another honeymoon couple like ourselves. That evening we met them on our way to our cabin and they said, 'Are you going ashore tomorrow at Gibraltar?'

'No, I don't think we will as we did so a year past January, but good luck to you.'

We saw them again the next evening after they had returned from their Rock visit. They approached us and said, 'We thought you were on your honeymoon like us until you said that you had visited Gibraltar eighteen months ago. We were married last Friday.' Then there followed a long tale in which it transpired that her parents had a job in Cuba and how difficult it had been for them trying to fix all the arrangements from that distance. They thought that they had booked Sunderland House for the reception only to find that someone had got in front of them. Their agent had tried to get the other party to change but they would not. We then disclosed that we too had been married on Friday and were the party who would not give way over Sunderland House and discovered that he and I had been at Cargilfield prep. school together. We also found out he had been reading *Alice in Wonderland* to his bride. On returning home we found the announcements of our two weddings side by side in the paper. Their name was Thorburne-Brown, and he, poor man, was killed in the war.

We arrived at Palma the morning after leaving Gibraltar and hired a car to drive us to our hotel which was on the far north-west side of the island. Our hotel, the Formentor, was the most modern and most luxurious. It certainly was large and new and we had good accommodation and very good service which was not surprising as we and a German honeymoon couple were the only people in the hotel. The weather was cold and so was the sea so we quickly got bored. We managed to find accommodation back in Palma and transferred back there. There we visited Mrs Cecil Aldin, widow of the well known painter of dogs. Mr Devitt had known Cecil Aldin before he went to live in Palma. One evening we went to watch a game of paluto – what a fast game, and what gambling went on.

It was soon time for us to return home and this we did by boat and train through France. We spent just one night at Longspring Wood before taking the night train back to Kirkcaldy. I had left the Bentley at Robb's garage and he brought it to the train for us. On arrival at Lahill it was my job to carry Ursula over the threshold and there was Mother to break a shortbread over her head. We were *home*.

# CHAPTER 14

# The start of married life

Lahill was the most attractive place. The house was situated on a small plateau with two grass parks, one on either side of the drive. There was a lodge cottage in which Robert, who was already married, was housed. The front door faced west and on the right of it there was a large drawing-room with a big window facing south, and another large window to the west. Behind there was a smoking-room of almost the same size, also with a bow window facing south. On the left of the front door was the dining-room with the kitchens and so on beyond that. The stair was wooden and had no carpet which made it very slippery. Behind the house was the garage, stabling for three horses, a room for the oil engine which made the light and a bothy for a groom. Behind that again there was a deep wooded den with a small burn running through it. There was a path through the den and on to the walled garden. There must have been fully an acre within the wall and it all sloped slightly to the south, altogether an ideal garden site if only it had been closer to the house. The gardener's house was at the top of the garden and was occupied by Bennett. He was a splendid man and we became very fond of him. In the parks there were trees and round the outside there was a strip of woodland which gave one complete privacy.

One of our first tasks was to find a small car for Ursula as without one she was very isolated. We landed up with a brand new small Wolseley Hornet. I think it was the very first morning that I left Ursula alone that Bennett came up to get orders from Madam.

After a short chat he finished by saying, 'I'll be needing a besom heed.'

'A what?' replied Ursula, completely mystified and not a little surprised. Ursula had only heard the term besom as a not very complementary term for a girl. 'You had better speak to my husband about that in the morning.'

He then explained that it was a new head for his brush that he required and from that moment on they were the best of friends.

Bennett also looked after the engine which made the light. I think it was only days after our arrival that he came to me and reported that the engine had broken down; I went to have a look at it with him and it had indeed broken down, the whole cylinder block was shattered. It was obvious that this was a major calamity. I got in touch with Mr Sutherland, the factor, who lived quite near. He came along and agreed that it was either a new engine or bringing in the power. He was not prepared to make a decision without first contacting Tommy and K who were both in Turkey. First he had to obtain estimates and then they had to go to Turkey by sea mail. After some weeks the reply came that the power should be installed. This meant obtaining way leaves for the lines etc., and so we were without light for four months. As the breakdown took place about the end of November we were without light all over our first Christmas. Fortunately it did not affect the central heating, but we had to go and buy lamps and candles. It took Ursula a long time to get used to going up to bed with a candle; she would always open the doors too quickly and out went the candle. I had learnt the art at Glenshirra.

Ursula had to start building a new social life. She had met a few people on her various visits to Leslie which gave her a starting-off point. As the latest newly-weds we were asked out to dinner and to cocktail parties quite frequently, but there was still in vogue, especially amongst the more elderly ladies, the system of calling. The procedure was for the local lady to call on the newcomer in the afternoon. If you were in you had a little chat and then Madam left, leaving three calling cards, two of her husband's and one of hers. If you were not in, the cards were left. The next step was for you to return the call, armed with your three cards. The great advantage of this system was that you had a record of names and addresses. As a newcomer you could not visit someone you did not know; the first move had to come from them.

The first major social event was the Leslie House Christmas Eve Dance. This was followed by the Fife Hunt Ball and both gave me a chance to show off my bride, and helped her to get to know several more people.

We started to attend Newburn parish church which was only about half a mile away. It was a typical small Scottish Presbyterian church, rectangular in shape. Inside it cannot have been more than 45 ft by 30 ft. The long south wall was divided in three by two tall windows, the centre space being occupied by the pulpit. Opposite the pulpit there were two boxes behind which there were two pews. There were also pews facing the pulpit at either end. There was a small gallery directly opposite the pulpit in which was the Lahill pew. The Rev. Neil was the minister and a very popular and kind man he was. Ursula had some difficulty finding her way round the Scottish Hymnary and he used to wait until she had found the place before finishing the announcement of it and allowing the organ to start.

One Sunday there was a large lady sitting in the pew immediately behind the box below us. Suddenly she fainted and slipped down, finishing up with her feet under the seat of the box in front of her. The service stopped and I rushed down and joined the rescue party. The pews were very narrow and it was some time before we managed to extract her. Once carried outside into the fresh air she soon revived and medical help was not required.

That church has now been converted into a private house by Tom and Jean Bingham.

Our first visitor was, not surprisingly, Sheila, Ursula's twin sister, who came to stay for the twins' birthday on 19 December.

Thereafter visitors came and went with fair regularity. Once the light was installed, my in-laws came to stay and they were followed by Sheila, accompanied by Mike Harrison to whom she had recently announced her engagement.

Some time before our wedding I had started looking for a groom. I was anxious to find a young man experienced enough to teach Ursula to ride and capable of breaking young horses. I contacted Mick Lindsay who, as a regular cavalry officer, was at that time involved in a riding school. I thought he might know of some suitable man who was leaving the services and was looking for a job in civvy street. He came back with the name of Sergeant Hodgson and told me that he had given him my address and told him to apply to me. We corresponded, came to terms and fixed a starting date on our return from honeymoon.

On Sergeant Hodgson's arrival I was immediately taken by him. He was a typical cavalry soldier: short, very black hair and a cheery smile.

We set up the stable at Lahill and brought Bandmaster over from Leslie. I had already asked Patrick, the posting master in Cupar, to look out for a horse suitable for Ursula to learn to ride on and suitable to carry a side saddle. He produced a mare called Madam, who was also installed at Lahill, and Ursula started to ride. Except for a few rides as a child she had no knowledge of horses. She worked hard and started coming out hunting. I don't think she was really enjoying it, but wanted to please me and keep her end up with the locals.

About the end of February I said to Hodgson, 'It is time we started getting Bandmaster fit for the Fife point-to-point.' I started riding at 6.30 every morning, back at eight o'clock for a quick breakfast and off to the factory. I entered Bandmaster in the welterweight and farmers' race, as I was riding Father's horse Red Hugh in the members' race. In those days it was a once round course and after the first couple of fields we jumped onto and off the public road just east of Balcormo Mains. I came in third on Red Hugh,

Bandmaster.

but when Bandmaster came to this obstacle he leapt onto the road and immediately turned right as home was not too far away in that direction. I was able to complete the circle and, jumping off the road, set off after the field. We managed to overhaul them all and we won the race.

At the races someone suggested that we should go to Ireland for the Punchistown Races. The idea appealed to me because I had never been, but also because I knew that the sales were on at Ballsbridge at the same time and I was keen to buy a young unbroken horse to follow Bandmaster and to give Hodgson something to do during the summer, breaking it. Guided by Patrick from Cupar I bought an unbroken four-year-old filly called Battlelight. Patrick arranged the transport for me and I arranged for Hodgson to meet her off the train. When I got home from Kirkcaldy on the

date of her arrival she was in the stable and I was met by Hodgson
with the remark, 'What's this bag of bones you have been buying?'
'You wait and see,' I replied.

Certainly she was small, only 15½ hands, rough-coated and thin,
having been running out all winter. She turned into a super mare
and later brood mare.

When we went to Lahill we knew that it could only be a
temporary home so we started looking for somewhere to buy.
Nothing turned up, so Father suggested first to Ursula and then to
me that if we would be prepared to live on Leslie Estate he would
build us a house, also houses for Robert and Hodgson. We agreed
and Alfred Scott of St Andrews was asked to prepare plans. It was
not long before we found a perfect site on Balgeddie Farm on the
foothills of the Lomond Hills, with a beautiful view over Leslie
House and the Leven valley. Father decided on the basic size of the
house but we were given every opportunity to make suggestions,
especially on internal details. Work must have started before the
end of 1936. It included not only a garage for three cars and a bothy
for a gardener but a garden with a 9 ft. garden wall of some forty
yards on the north side and thirty yards on the east side. I never
realised at the time what a large project it was.

Very early in our married life we acquired a delightful Lakeland
terrier, whom we christened Daniel, but unfortunately his life was
short as he died of distemper. There was no means of immunisation
available in those days. So there we were, dog hunting again, when
we saw an advertisement in The Times for a wolfhound in
Maidenhead. We wrote off to inquire about him and received the
most lengthy reply from his lady owner. We learnt that his name
was Fergus of Culafin and that his father had defended his mistress
from a lion in Kenya. We fell and sent off our cheque and he arrived
by train. He was not exactly a show dog as he was too small and
not too true on his fore legs, but in every other way he was a
lovely dog.

Soon after their visit to us Mike and Sheila announced that their wedding was to be on 26 July, just when I was to be at TA camp. The date was in fact only two days before camp finished and I managed to get excused the last two days so that I could attend the wedding. Ursula decided that she would go south the night before I went to camp and stay at Longspring Wood until after the wedding and that we could return together. Fergus was to be left in the house with the staff to look after him.

When the day came we put all the luggage in the car and then went in to say goodbye but there was no sign of Fergus. As we had a train to catch we just had to go, but when we got into the car there he was on the back seat. We did not have the heart to throw him out and Ursula said if they would let him on the train she would take him with us, and that is exactly what happened. I think my in-laws were a little surprised when he arrived but took it very well. My father-in-law got Wail, the garden handyman, to erect a six foot wire enclosure in which Fergus was to be put for the day of the wedding. I arrived on the morning of the wedding to be picked up by the faithful Mathew at Kings Cross. When we were all ready to leave for the church Fergus was put in his enclosure and off we went. When we returned there was Fergus standing on the front doorstep preventing entry to those who had come direct to the house. He was soon back in our bedroom and all was well.

About the middle of October we dashed up to Struy to get a day or two stalking before the end of the season. I think it must have been the last day we were coming down the Black Bridge path when Ursula reported that all was not well with her. We continued slowly to the bottom where fortunately there was a glen telephone on which we could summon a car. It took a considerable time before the car arrived and when we got back to the lodge Ursula was put to bed and the doctor summoned. Dr Munroe diagnosed a threatened miscarriage and said that she must stay in bed and not put a foot to the ground.

The next day the family left for Fife and we were left behind. After about two weeks the doctor said that Ursula could travel south if she went by train so I put her on the train in Inverness and met her off it in Perth. Fortunately all went well from then on, but it did mean no more riding which I think was secretly welcomed. As a result of our delayed return from Struy we missed my brother Frank's wedding. He married Isobel Chadwick, a distant relation of my mother's from Canada. She was a very pretty girl who had stayed with us at Leslie on a number of occasions.

From now on the planning and building of Balgeddie was to take much of our spare time. Tradesmen had to be selected and Alex Fraser of Kirkcaldy, who had built many of the Nairn factories in Kirkcaldy, were the builders. Black of Kirkcaldy were the plumbers and Martins the electricians. The joiners were Thom of St Andrews. In those days Thos. Ward operated a large ship-breaking yard at Inverkeithing. It was their practice when a liner came in to hold an auction of all fittings etc. As it happened, the RMS *Homeric* had just come in. She was originally a German liner which had been taken over by the British as reparations after the First World War. We bought part of B deck as flooring for all the main rooms in Balgeddie, and what splendid floors it made.

Now that the location of our home was fixed at Leslie it was obvious that we would require transport for horses. I looked around and found a four-wheel three horse trailer. It was clear that neither the Bentley or the Wolseley were capable of pulling such a vehicle, so the Wolseley went and was replaced by a Ford Utility with a V8 engine. It was built in Canada and had a wooden body and three rows of seats, the back two rows of which could be removed. It ran all through the war and for several years after and finally finished with a roof rack and capable of carrying four children, nanny, a large dog and all the luggage to Struy. The trailer was in use until I gave up hunting on moving to West Hall in 1966.

When point-to-point time came round again I asked Father if I

could take Red Hugh over to Lahill and get him fit along with
Bandmaster. One day, unbeknown to me, Hodgson invited Robert
the butler, who did not ride, to ride one of the horses up to
Gilston to the blacksmith. All went well on the way up, so Hodgson suggested that Robert should take Red Hugh home as he was
finished and that he would wait for the other one. No one really
knows what followed but it appears that Red Hugh took command and on coming to a sharp left turn, round he went but
Robert went straight on. Red Hugh was home first without either
party receiving serious injury. When the race day came I was
lucky as I won the first race on Bandmaster and the last race on
Red Hugh.

We were expecting the arrival of our first child early in June
and Mrs Devitt and a charming young monthly nurse called Agnes
Wright arrived towards the end of May. Expectation grew but
nothing happened. However Fergus, the dog, cut his leg rather
badly. 'That needs a stitch,' said Nurse, 'I will do it,' so she
produced the necessary from her kit and with Ursula and me
holding the dog proceeded to make a perfect job. There followed
much walking, then finally things really seemed to be on the move
and Dr Bonar was summoned. Again there was disappointment
and Dr Bonar gave Ursula a sleeping pill and said he did not
expect anything till the next day. Ursula went to sleep and I went
off to my bed.

I woke early and as all was quiet, I went out to paint some trees
to prevent the horses barking them. I had just started when I
heard a shout from Nurse from the window, 'Come quick, I need
your help.'

I immediately downed tools, rushed inside and after a quick
wash dashed upstairs. 'Here, hold this, do that,' and before I knew
where I was I was acting as assistant midwife. I had arrived just
as the baby was born, a little blueish girl. All this was very new
to Ursula but not quite so to me as I had been at the births
of several lambs, calves and foals. However all went well and

Nurse proved to be most capable and fully in control, and so on 13 June we started our parenthood. Four days later my mother-in-law returned south. On 10 July Nurse Wright left and Nanna Rattray arrived. The former had been a tower of strength and had given us a wonderful start. Nanna Rattray's father was a stationmaster in Fife, but they came originally from Loch Carron, and what a nice family they were. Almost immediately Sarah Ursula was christened at Lahill by the Rev. Willie McCraw. Ursula, Sarah and Nanna then left for Longspring Wood and I went off to camp.

Ursula with Sarah.

Balgeddie was growing fast but there was still a lot to do. In September Isobel gave birth to their first, also a daughter, Susan. I remember we looked into their house in Cupar to see the baby on our way to Struy. Frank and Isobel planned to take over the lease of Lahill when we moved to Balgeddie. For some reason or other they wanted to do this sooner than expected and Balgeddie was not ready so we agreed to move to stay with my parents at Leslie House until it was.

As Christmas approached we too were anxious to get into our new home so we planned to move in on the Saturday before Christmas although there was no front door or front staircase.

The staff were moved in; Ursula moved up on the Saturday morning and I planned to follow on returning from hunting. It snowed before I got back and I could not get the trailer up the hill so I had to unload the horses at the bottom and walk them up. Now we were in and a new era was starting.

# CHAPTER 15

# The start at Balgeddie

Early the next week it was Christmas Day and as was the wont in Scotland it was not a holiday. The joiners arrived and I went off to Kirkcaldy. I did however return for lunch. Ursula had organised a Christmas cake and we all, the staff included, joined the joiners in a cup of tea. The foreman joiner made a speech welcoming us into our new house and wishing us all happiness. What a super start to life at Balgeddie! About a week later it was Hunt Ball time and our first Balgeddie guests arrived. We still had no front stair, but what did that matter?

In the field in which we had chosen to build there was a relatively flat area approximately 150 yards from north to south and 400 yards from east to west, after which it fell away sharply giving us our lovely view. There were hedges on either side with a row of hedgerow trees. This area was fenced off as our garden and the building contractor levelled an area in front of the house for a lawn. It was obvious that we must have a gardener to build our garden and we found a young man called Thomson who had served his time, and he set to work with a will. The lawn was sown, hedges were planted and fruit trees bought for the garden wall. Soon things began to take shape.

The house was quite large, rectangular in shape, with the long sides to the south and north. The front door was approximately in the centre of the north side and led into a wide lobby which in turn led into the long hall which ran the full length of the house and was about twelve feet wide. At the west end of the hall there was a door into the garden. In the south-west corner was a large drawing-room with a bow window to the south and a window to the west. Next was a smoking-room with a door to the garden, and then the dining-room. On the north side there was a flower-cum-gun-room, the gents' cloakroom, the front door, the stair and a bedroom with a bath and loo.

In the south-east corner of the hall there was a swing door to the back. On the right through this door there was the butler's pantry and then a large servants' hall, whose windows had to face east so that they could not see us on the lawn opposite. There was the back stair which went both up and down to the boiler room where there were two boilers, one for central heating and the other for the hot water. Each boiler had its own mechanical stoker which required granulated coal; they were very efficient and left practically no ash. Coal was much cheaper than oil as there was lots of it and at the time no North Sea oil. Next to the stair was the back door, then came the scullery and a large kitchen. After that was a loo, a storeroom, and a larder. Then there was a block which ran north and contained a door to the garden, a laundry backed by a greenhouse, then a coal-house backed by a potting shed. Next was the garage for three cars and finally the gardener's bothy with bath and loo, and a garage workshop.

Upstairs we had the master suite of bedroom, bathroom and dressing room. There followed on the south side two bedrooms, a night nursery, day nursery and nursery bathroom. On the north side there was a bathroom and a large hanging cupboard for Ursula's dresses. Then came the stair and another bedroom. Through a door there was a linen room, stair up to the attic, four bedrooms, bath and loo, and an ironing room. In the attic there was a changing room for the butler and a large open space used for storage and later a children's playroom. So there we were in this beautiful new house with one child, a nanny, a butler, a cook, a house-maid, a between maid, a gardener and a groom.

In May my sister Matilda married Captain Ronnie Richards, a

Cambridge friend of Douglas, in Christ's Kirk on the Green, Leslie.

By now we knew that number two was expected in July. Various visitors came and went including my in-laws. Before we knew where we were it was July and Nursie Lobban had arrived. She was a stout grey-haired lady, but a great character and sport. As the days ticked over she could be seen out on the lawn bent double digging out weeds. I think camp must have been at Annsmuir that year as I managed to be at home on the day of the birth. Our doctor was Dr Maitland (Randy). He was a local man and was married to a local girl, Barbara Wemyss. Their birthdays are only days apart and they are now both ninety-three or -four now. On this occasion I was given a hand pump which was supposed to deliver some form of anaesthetic. I pumped like mad to no effect, only to find that there was a kink in the pipe. Eventually a boy was delivered and we had our son and heir, Ian.

We now settled down to consolidate the position; there was much to do. Lahill had been only partially furnished so we were a bit short on furniture. By visiting the many antique shops round the East Neuk we slowly collected quite nice pieces at very modest prices. There was much to do in the garden too. On one occasion Ursula and I dug up some silver birches in one of the Leslie woods. They are now a row of elegant trees.

While things were going well for us personally, the news from Europe continued to deteriorate and it looked as if war was not too far away. Neville Chamberlain went off to meet Hitler and we set off for Ireland. We planned a week's holiday sleeping in the Ford Utility from which we had removed the back seats. We had a lovely time travelling along the north coast and down the west as far as Achill Isle. The scenery was beautiful and life still very simple. We saw women dressed in red skirts with black shawls round their shoulders loading peats into panniers on little donkeys. We called at hotels each evening to hear the radio news in case the TA had been mobilised when I should have to return home. The

Ursula's presentation.

Munich agreement was signed however and we finished our holiday.

Back in Kirkcaldy there were more signs of war. The company chemists were working full out with the Ministry of Defence to produce a gas-proof fabric. The research was a success and later production reached a million yards a week.

Christmas came and went followed by a large party for the Hunt Ball.

In March there was more pomp and ceremony as my mother decided that she would like to present her daughter Matilda and her two daughters-in-law Ursula and Isobel on their marriages. I have never been quite sure what was achieved by these presentations, any more than what was achieved by being presented at a levée; however, it was a socially desirable thing to do. It took place about nine o'clock in the evening at Buckingham Palace. The ladies paraded in their best long gowns, bedecked in what jewels they had, with ostrich feathers on their heads, long white gloves and carrying fans. Males accompanying their wives or daughters wore full dress. On the throne on this occasion were King George VI and Queen Elizabeth, King George V having died when we were at Lahill. The men played no part in the procedure. We all assembled in a large hall and the ladies were marshalled into some sort of order waiting for their turn. When that moment came the ladies walked in, turned to face Their Majesties, curtsied first to the King then took two side steps, curtsied to the Queen, turned and walked out the other side. After presentation the ladies rejoined their escorts and we all went upstairs for refreshments. Finally the King and Queen arrived and spoke to a few people and then the party was over. Unfortunately, during this last stage Ursula did not feel well, feeling sick, but luckily she managed to last out.

In April my sister Clare married John Powell, a friend of John Gilmour who had joined the Fife and Forfar Yeo. This wedding was also in Christ's Kirk on the Green.

I won the members race on Battlelight: so much for Hodgson's 'bag of bones'.

Things were going from bad to worse in Europe and in April the Government decided to double the TA. As far as the F & F were concerned this meant our little Armoured Car Company being increased to two Armoured Regiments. Sandy McIntosh and I had the job to do in the Kirkcaldy area. Recruits poured in including a bunch from the Kirkcaldy Rugby Club; these ones nearly all got commissions but sadly they did not all return. Sandy's father was a doctor and vetted them as they came in.

They were marched in and stripped to the waist and he would say to them, 'Let me see you touch your toes; can you read this? OK, next one.' No one fell out as unfit. The Fife and Forfar were the first Regiment in Scotland to reach their target and the second in the UK. We went to camp at Catterick, but as far as I can remember the new recruits did not come.

Once again we decided to try and have that last holiday before war started and we booked into a hotel in Monte Carlo for two weeks. We flew out, starting from London Hendon, to Paris where we changed to a French plane. We were scheduled to have one stop *en route* and when that moment arrived and we were making our approach the co-pilot, a bearded man, came down the cabin and stopping quite near my seat began lifting the carpet.

'What are you doing?' I asked.

'Well, we have a little problem with the undercarriage so I am going to screw them down by hand.'

He lifted a small door in the floor and then, with what looked like a wheel brace, proceeded to screw them down. We had no further problem.

We arrived at, I say Cannes, Ursula says Marseilles, and drove by car the rest of the way. Our first week was beautiful and I started to learn to water-ski. The weather then broke and France declared general mobilisation. This meant that all the members of their conscript army had to report to their regiments.

We decided to return home, but how? There was no way we could get a flight so we opted for the train. Fortunately the train started from Menton, so we registered our baggage through to Balgeddie and boarded the train with a paper bag with Ursula's best hat, a sponge bag and a razor. We had arrived at the station very early and got two seats. Quite some time before the train was due to start it was packed with people standing in the corridors. Suddenly an American popped his head into our compartment and said quietly to us, 'We have only two "Froggies" in our compartment, would you like to swap with them?' This we did willingly as our lot were reeking of garlic. We trundled along slowly with people even climbing in through the windows whenever we stopped.

After about twelve hours we arrived in Paris where we found a young British couple trying to get home. We suggested that they join us and we would take a taxi to our next station. We boarded the Blue Train for which we should have had booked seats and sat down in the first seats we found. When the ticket holders arrived we apologised and moved on, eventually landing up in the diner. After a good breakfast we were pushed out of there and landed up in a luggage rack. The boat was absolutely packed; we were one of the last to get on and just had to stand at the top of the gangway for the whole voyage. Fortunately the sea was a dead calm, and, being last on, we were first off and got a seat on the train up to London. We managed to get a sleeper that night for Kirkcaldy. Quite remarkably, all our luggage, including tennis racquets, arrived within a day or two.

# CHAPTER 16

# The War starts

On 1 September 1939 the TA was mobilised and we became full time soldiers. On paper the 1st and 2nd Fife and Forfar were separate regiments but on the ground we still occupied the same premises. Sandy McIntosh became Colonel of the Second with Fergus McIntyre as second in command, Andrew Brown got A squadron, John Gilmour B and me C squadron.

On the first Sunday I held a squadron church parade. Dressed in our new battle dress we marched up the street to St Brydesdale church where the Rev. Macdonald-Ross was the minister. We filled the front rows and the service began. I cannot remember at what point it was but the siren for an air raid sounded. As senior officer what should I do? Should I confer with the minister, should I order a dispersal? No, I thought, the old British practice of the stiff-upper-lip was the line to take so we all sat still and Mr Macdonald-Ross continued. A fireman then came in and placed a piece of paper in front of the minister. He took no notice and, following our example, just carried on. Finally he picked up the paper and read out, 'There has been an air raid warning and all congregations are advised to disperse.' Just at that moment the All Clear sounded.

Quite soon we learnt that the Regiment was to be billeted on Leslie and Markinch and that C Squadron were to be in the town hall and Christ's Kirk hall. As we had no transport we were ordered to march. Not on the hard road I thought, we will go across country. So up Johnnie Marshall's loan we went and, using

Myself in 1940.

various old rights of way, we arrived. I could not believe my luck: I was able to sleep at home as it took me less than five minutes to get down from there.

All good things had to come to an end and after a very cold Christmas we left by train for Beaumont barracks, Aldershot where we took over from the first regiment who had been posted to France. Quite soon I discovered that one of the Younger family had a furnished house in Fleet which they were prepared to let to us. Ursula and the children moved in. My problem was that I had no transport by which to get back and forth, so I bought a second-hand motor-bike. This magnificent machine was called an OK Supreme and I had it until after the war. The regiment moved out to Farnham which made the bike even more helpful.

In June we were on the move again and our destination was supposed to be secret but somehow it leaked out that it was to be Northern Ireland. We travelled by train to Stranraer, crossed by ferry and boarded another train for Dungannon. We, the officers, travelled in what must have been a Royal Coach. It was a big open coach with the walls all covered in pink silk and had armchairs to sit on. All went well till we failed to make the top of a hill just short of Dungannon. We reversed back and had another attempt. We were of course all looking out of the windows and shouting words of encouragement. Suddenly we saw the fireman bashing the side of the engine with a long-handled hammer. It transpired that he was trying to release sand to give the engine a better grip. Even with all his efforts we failed again. It had been decided to cut the train in half when suddenly a second engine appeared. It pushed from behind and we made the top.

We received a most warm welcome and soon began to make friends. It was not long before some of us began to look for homes for our wives. I found two elderly spinster sisters called Macmannus, who owned a slightly larger house. They said that they would move to the top of the house and leave us the bottom with the children. They even put in electric light for us. We kept in touch with them for some years after the war.

The Presbyterian minister, the Rev. Thomson, was a great help and many a happy evening was spent by groups of troopers in his manse. Social life developed very well and several soldiers and some wives even joined the local drama group. In fact life was very comfortable. In spite of this however we did work hard especially at our map reading in case we strayed over the border and got interned for the duration. Security was very tight as there were a few IRA about and all weapons had to be locked up when not carried. It got even tighter after an incident at Ballykinler camp, some miles from us. The camp was being enlarged and there were many contractors working in the place. One day at lunch time a lorry drove up to the armory, seized the single guard, and with his keys proceeded to load all the rifles onto their lorry. They then drove off taking the guard with them. They released him in Belfast and he rang the camp and discovered that no one had even realised he was missing.

As the months passed we were all looking forward to a happy Christmas when a blow fell. We received orders to move to Besbrook on 19 December.

Ursula and I were invited to a farewell dinner party by Colonel Stevenson, the Mayor of Dungannon, and while at table the maid came in and placed what looked like a telegram in front of him. After reading it he handed it to me and it read, 'The GOC is pleased that the regiment has endeared itself to the people of Dungannon but regret that the move cannot be altered as it involves other units,' or words to that effect. It transpired that on learning of the move the local council had sent a telegram to Winston Churchill, the Secretary of State for War and GOC Northern Ireland District, asking for the move to be put off until after Christmas so that the men could enjoy all the Christmas dinners planned for them. We moved to Besbrook but had an exercise which landed up in Dungannon on Christmas Day.

This move meant that I should have to find a new home for Ursula and the children. If I failed she would have to return to Scotland. Once again I was lucky and I found rooms in a large house called Drumalane, part of which was already occupied by an officer from a Welsh infantry regiment. We had two large rooms and, I think, two small bedrooms and an improvised kitchen. We were told by the caretaker that our bedroom had not been used for years so it was very cold, and the fire could not be lit as it smoked so badly. We started to explore and found in an attic what looked like a soot box in what we thought was the offending chimney. We opened it and extracted two large sackfuls of sticks and other jackdaw nest materials; once this was removed the chimney worked beautifully.

We did not have long to enjoy our new home as the army decided that they wanted the building as an officers' mess, so once again we were house hunting. We found an elderly lady who said she would take us in. It was to be a tight squeeze but as her sister had gone into a home it would be possible. We learnt that the sister had been jilted in youth and had taken to her bedroom from which she had never emerged till she was taken to the home.

I think it was about this time that Nanna Rattray decided that she must leave and do something of greater help to the war effort. She left and trained as a State Registered Nurse. After the war she became a health visitor and finally a supervisor. We still keep in touch with her in her retirement home at Loch Carron. It was just about this time that I got a week's leave so we left Sarah and Ian with my sister Clare who had a house called Greenbushes. We flew to Liverpool, trained to London, and then took another train to Fife. We had hardly arrived at Balgeddie when I received a signal to report forthwith to the Senior Officers School at Devizes for a course which was t) last several weeks. We decided that Ursula would return to Ireland, collect the children and bring them back to Balgeddie.

I must turn aside now to record her exploits over the next week or so. We knew that Harry Melville, one of my subalterns, was on leave in Kirkcaldy and Ursula thought that it would be much nicer to travel back with him than alone. Ursula wanted to fly but Harry only had a warrant to travel by sea. He suggested that he could organise for her to travel on his warrant if she was prepared to travel as Mrs Melville, and this she agreed to do. They had not been long at sea when the alarm sounded and they were all assembled on deck. They wondered what the casualty list would show if the worst happened. Harry was not married and Ursula was not on board.

The return journey was even more dramatic. She was not keen to take the children by sea so she arranged to put the car on the boat, stay the night in Belfast and fly over in the morning, by which time the car should be in Glasgow. The loading of the car and the night in Belfast went fine but in the morning it was announced that owing to a heavy air raid on Glasgow the plane could not get over. They said that they hoped it would be OK for the following morning and confirmed with Ursula that she wished to go.

Next morning they boarded the plane and Ursula had a young naval officer sitting directly behind her. She asked him if he would help her with the children if the flight was rough; this he willingly agreed to do and tapped her on the shoulder every few minutes to check that all was well. When it was about time to land, the plane began doing some rather queer things and Ursula thought she heard morse code. Eventually they landed but not at the right airport. It was an RAF aerodrome and they were caught up in an air raid. It was announced that service personnel could go to the officers' mess but that civilians must stay on the plane. It turned out that Ursula and the children were the only civilians so they sat in the plane alone listening to gunfire and getting very hot in the sun. The door was only some five feet from the ground and everyone had jumped out so Ursula thought that a little fresh air would be nice. She lowered the children to the ground and jumped down herself. After playing around for a little she noticed people returning to the plane and she popped the children in but could not make it herself, it was just too high. Steps were produced and everyone boarded. They then sat for some time as one of the engines would not start. Eventually they were told that they would be taken into Glasgow by bus.

On arrival Ursula's naval friend went with her to find the car, only to find that it had not been unloaded and could not be until the next high tide. The day was now well spent and she could not wait that long with the children. She decided to seek the help of her Uncle Charlie, Captain Woollcombe RN, who was in charge of the docks. The party went off and found him. Ursula expected to receive a warm welcome. In fact she received a very cool reception and was told most firmly that she should get out of Glasgow as quick as possible. What should she do? Her naval friend said he was going to Edinburgh if that was any help. By this time Ursula was getting short of cash, having had to spent an extra night in Belfast, so she asked if she could, travel on his warrant. 'I expect so,' he replied and off they went as Lt. and Mrs ? to Edinburgh where they parted and Ursula and children continued to Kirkcaldy from where she telephoned my Father who sent a car for her. The next day Father sent Geordie Brown to Glasgow to fetch the car and so ended an eventful round trip.

Quite soon Ursula travelled south to spend a few week with her sister Sheila and Mike at Witheypool in Devonshire. There they were within striking distance of where I was and I was able to spend two short weekends with them.

At the end of my course I returned to Ireland. During the year in Ireland there had been quite a number of changes in personnel. Several NCOs had gone to OCTU, some had returned to the regiment on being commissioned while others found places in other regiments. Of the officers, Andrew Brown left first, followed by Jo Grimond; but the one that affected us most was the promotion of Sandy McIntosh, who had commanded the regiment since it was formed. He left early in December to become second in command of a brigade. Later he became CO of the Phantom Regiment, about which we may hear more later. Fergus filled the gap until our new CO arrived, Lt. Col. Sword (Scabbard to most people). He came from the 13–18th Hussars and was the most delightful chap. He was, I am sure, a fine horseman and cavalry soldier but he was quite unsuited for a mechanised regiment.

On one occasion there was a large exercise, or TEWT, involving the whole of Northern Ireland, but each regiment was represented only by a single staff car. It was to be a twenty-four-hour performance. I got the job of acting second in command to Colonel Sword. We travelled in a large Humber staff car fitted with blinds all round for black-out; it had a partition across the middle also fitted with a blind. Some time early in the morning – it was summer so got light early – we were standing outside our car chatting when I noticed a party approaching in the distance. 'That looks like the General,' I said, whereupon Scabbard jumped into the car, pulled down the blinds and shouted to me, 'Tell him I am not here.' He then slammed the door. That was one of my more difficult chats with the General; I doubt if I convinced him.

About June we received word that we would be returning to the mainland, leaving our vehicles behind. We were to be re-equipped as an armoured regiment. We moved to Whitby in July.

When we arrived in Whitby we had no vehicles of any sort, but slowly Matilda and Valentine tanks began to arrive and drivers, gunners and wireless operators began their training. Someone had the brilliant idea that it would be a good plan for the troop leaders to receive some training on cross country manoeuvering and the use of ground generally. I got the job and a small camp was set up on the Yorkshire Moors not far from the beautiful little village of Goathland. All training had to be done on foot, and they came in batches while I stayed there all the time. A local farmer lent me a pony from which I could command my forces. This was a great help to me. As winter approached we began to move into winter quarters in the town, and it was again possible for Ursula to join me.

Soon after arriving in Whitby, Colonel Sword left us and was replaced by Colonel Cooper of the 3rd Tanks. The next one to go was Fergus McIntyre, the oldest serving officer left in the regiment. That left me in that position.

After a very cold winter the regiment was mobile again and started serious training on the Yorkshire moors.

In early summer Ursula returned to Scotland as we were on the move again. We moved to Stanmer Park, Brighton and trained on the Downs. One amusing incident happened at the end of a three-day brigade exercise. I think we must have been told to tune in to the brigade net to hear the Brigadier's comments on how it had gone. There we all were silently waiting for the big man to speak when we were astonished to hear the following: 'There's Wee Brucie got Mathers picking Fleurs to 'im.' There was no disguising from which regiment that had come, and from whose squadron. The poor man thought he was speaking on his tank intercom to another member of the crew.

In October we moved to Bury St Edmunds for training in

different country, and once again we had a new CO, Lt. Col. Alex Scott. After a summer at home Ursula joined me at Bury St Edmunds. It was while in Bury that I mounted the OK Supreme with Ursula on the pillion and off we went to Newmarket to watch the St Ledger. All Classic races were run at Newmarket during the war.

After a month or so at Bury we moved to Chippenham Park, Newmarket. After a short sojourn in a hotel we found lodgings with a Mrs Leaf, quite close to Chippenham Park. She was a very tall lady with a son in Motor Torpedo Boats with Peter Scott and a daughter a ferry pilot flying bombers from America to the UK. As the children were really too much for Mrs Leaf we managed to lease Badlingham Manor, complete with cook. It was a lovely house with a moat round it and muskovy ducks. While we were at Chippenham John Gilmour and I shared a Nissan hut with a partition in the middle; he had one end and I the other. On Old Years Night I was sleeping out at Badlingham when the hut went up in flames. John escaped all right but we both lost all our clothes and camp equipment. We received a special clothing ration to replace our clothes and our two wives had a wonderful shopping spree in Cambridge buying us replacements.

From time to time there were rumours that we were going overseas and we even had forty-eight hour embarkation leave, but it came to nothing. Then things definitely seemed to be on the move and I set off in command of a train load of tanks with three other officers and two men per tank. During the night we officers were playing bridge when the train came to a stop in what appeared to be open country. After some time the guard came into our compartment and said to me, 'Could I have a word with you, please?' and he invited me out into the corridor. 'You are wanted on the telephone at the signal box.' It was very dark but we scrambled down onto the line and walked up to the signal box. There I was informed that our move was cancelled and that we were to return to camp. I did not know if this was an hoax or not. Anyway we could not go back down the up line so we had to go on to a station where we could cross to the down line. When we got to the station I rang Movement Control and confirmed the order. We were somewhere in Northumberland and the poor engine driver had to push this heavy train many miles to, I think, York where we could get an engine on the right end. The other ranks knew nothing of what was going on and when they found themselves back in Newmarket you should have heard their language.

We were granted a forty-eight hour leave and decided to go to London. We had to take the children with us as we had no one to leave them with. We could not get into Browns Hotel so landed up in the Ritz. Neither of us had ever stayed there before and when we were signing the register we heard a small but very clear voice say, 'Mummy, isn't this posh'! We had planned to go to a show the first night if we could find someone to look after the children. We thought we might get someone from an agency and asked the house-maid if she knew of any. 'I will look after them,' she said, and as she seemed such a nice woman we accepted her offer. The second night we took them to a pantomime; this was a great success except that Ian had to spend a penny about every twenty minutes.

About this time I was sent on a rather curious course at Bovington. There were, I think, five majors and about twenty captains on the course. We were made into five-man tank crews with all the majors in the same crew. In our case you were driver one day, co-driver the next, then gunner, radio operator, and regimental CO and tank commander. One of our number who was not keen to take his turn as driver, which included the dirty job of filling up and maintenance, went sick that day. Later in the war that man became my commanding officer. I enjoyed the course in spite of having to change a track bogie on a very wet and dark night.

In June we moved up to Bridlington in Yorkshire and Ursula returned home. I think it must have been about September that Ursula came down to Bridlington; what an easy war I was having. On one occasion we were returning from Balgeddie to Bridlington

and we had with us a very fussy governess called Miss Day. The
train at Kirkcaldy was packed; however, we had to get in. I pushed
Miss Day in followed by the two children, then Ursula, and finally
I had to get the porter to push me in. We travelled like that to
Edinburgh where we rushed off to look for seats on the next train.
We bundled into the first seats we found and then I went off to
see if there was more room elsewhere. I found an empty compartment and we moved, but Miss Day would not come. When lunch
time came we had the picnic lunch so we went to try and find Miss
Day, only to find that there was a locked door between her and us
so she had to go without her lunch. When we arrived at York,
where we had to change, we set off for the hotel as we had about
an hour to wait for the next train. Miss Day said she would not
come but would go and look for something to eat. When we
returned we found Miss Day in an even worse mood as there
was no food on the platform and the officials would not let her
off as we had her ticket. When we eventually arrived she
announced that she was sick so we had to put her to bed as well
as the children.

In January '44 we had another jaunt to London, this time for my
sister Margaret's wedding to Humphry Atkins, a young naval
officer. Ursula and my sister Clare, whose husband John Powell was
an officer in the regiment, decided to travel down together with the
children while John and I followed later. They had to change trains
at Scarborough and just as Ursula was about to board the second
train she noticed that she had lost a diamond brooch from her
blouse. She rushed into the RTO office and reported what had
happened and they said they would tell the police or keep it until
her return, should it be handed in. I don't remember much about
the wedding or the reception but in the evening we were to go out
to dinner, I think at the Berkeley. Once again the maid said she
would take the children to the shelter should the alarm sound, and
we said we would return if it did. This time the siren did sound and
we rushed back and joined the party in the shelter.

On our return to Bridlington Ursula went to the police about her brooch. Nothing had been handed in so she supplied a description of it with a sketch and it was agreed to put an advertisement in the local paper offering a reward. A week later Ursula was summoned to the police station and again asked to describe the brooch. It had been sent to the police in a match box with the label in block letters and no name. She was lucky to get it back.

In February I received what I thought was a shattering blow. I was summoned to the CO's office and informed that I was to be transferred to the Staffordshire Yeomanry under an exchange system ordered by Monty. I was informed that I could take my batman with me. We organised for Ursula to return to Balgeddie and I proceeded to report to my new unit at Gordonstoun School near Elgin.

I need not have worried as I received a wonderful welcome from all ranks from the Colonel down. I took over A Squadron from Major Nicoll who took my place. Our main task was to practise beach landings from landing craft. As it appeared that we would be there for some weeks Ursula joined me and we lived in a hotel in Elgin. Our bedroom was over a baker's shop and was over-run with mice so we bought a mouse trap and had caught about twelve in quick succession before we gave up. While in Elgin the children, who were just recovering from whooping-cough, learnt to ride bicycles.

In the end of March we moved down to our concentration area at Haywards Heath. For some reason or other I had to do that journey in a jeep in one day with my new driver Davies. What a nice chap he was and we did a lot more long journeys together. I must jump back for a minute: when we were mobilised, Robert Redpath our butler joined up as my batman, but it was not long before he was pinched to become officers' mess sergeant. I asked for volunteers from the squadron and selected Percy Henderson. He remained with me until the war ended. He became very fond of our children and was very good with them. He died about two years ago.

In the assembly area, the main concentration was on tuning up and waterproofing our vehicles, although we did have some tactical exercises. We also had to programme in a forty-eight-hour leave for everyone. Ursula and I met in London and had it not been for that leave Catriona would not have arrived when she did. Before the end of the month our camps were sealed and no one and no letters were allowed out. As a squadron leader I always seemed to be at some planning meeting or sand table exercise. The detailed planning was most meticulously done. As 'D Day' approached we moved down to Stanmer Park from where we loaded onto our little tank landing craft at Newhaven. Each craft carried a cross-section of all arms so that if one was sunk it did not make too big a hole in any one unit. The senior army officer was in command of all troops and he was given a sort of Father Christmas bag containing all the detailed orders for all units on the ship. This sealed bag was not to be opened until a code word was received. As far as we were concerned all communication was through our regimental net, but of course there was wireless silence until the code was received. Our naval crew were two, both of whom looked incredibly young. The captain was a lieutenant and the other a midshipman. They were a charming and very efficient pair.

We were already loaded when we received the message that there was to be a twenty-four-hour postponement. For security we were not allowed off the ship and spent a very uncomfortable night with nothing but the deck to lie down on and minimal cooking and other facilities. Early next morning we were allowed on shore for an hour during which to take exercise but we were not allowed outside the dock gates. I knew that we had to sail by 4.00 p.m. if we were to get down the coast in time to take our place in the main fleet emerging from Southampton. This time it came and off we went.

I had been issued with special sea sick pills with strict instructions on how to administer them. Although the official weather was rough seas, I don't remember it being so or having many demands for pills. It was dark by the time we took our place in the convoy. How our skipper found it I don't know, but we spent the night following a little red light on the stern of the boat in front. When dawn broke, what an amazing sight! There were craft in all directions and most of us were carrying a barrage balloon to prevent low flying enemy aircraft. Somehow our balloon got semi-deflated and became dangerous and we had to cut it adrift.

After a short delay we made an almost dry landing and were directed off the beach. We had got a certain distance inland when a fleet of RAF bombers arrived, then suddenly the sky was full of parachutes of every colour. The airborne division had landed by glider during the night and this was their equipment arriving. Later I was passing through a village when an old lady emerged, clapping her hands in welcome. Just at that moment three German prisoners came trotting down the road with their hands above their heads; she slapped each one across the face just to help them on their way.

My squadron had a pretty uneventful day except for Sergeant Joyce who could not believe his eyes when he saw four German tanks emerge from a wood, one behind the other. He skilfully waited until they were well in the open, when he bumped off the last one thereby blocking their escape route and then picked off the remaining three. When darkness came we were drawn back and so ended my first day in battle.

At night we dug two-foot deep slit trenches to sleep in. As long as you were below ground level you were fairly safe except from a direct hit. For some days after this we spent most of our time acting as additional artillery in support of the infantry. After about three weeks we had a day off and managed to get to a mobile bath unit where we were able to get our clothes off for the first time for about three weeks. My, was that shower good!

On 6 July we took part in the battle for Caen where once again I was lucky from the casualty point of view. On the 16th we moved to the east of the River Orne and took part in the battle for Falaise.

On the 25th we were pulled out and told that we were going home to be re-equipped with new amphibious equipment. We left our tanks behind, and sailing from Arromanches arrived at Newhaven on the 29th.

We went first to Stanmer Park, then on to a camp near Grimsby. HQ and C squadrons went on leave while A and B got stuck into training on our new swimming tanks. This included the use of Davies submarine escape apparatus.

While we were here, Colonel Eadie left the regiment for a staff job. We were all very sorry to see him go as he had commanded the regiment all through the desert and on to this moment. He was not only very efficient but also a delightful man. He could not have been kinder to me, an incomer. Mike Farquhar, the second in command, took over as Colonel. He too was a Yeoman and a very good soldier as well as being really nice. Ursula came down leaving the children with Ursula Gilmour who was staying at Balgeddie, and we returned together when our leave turn came.

The Regiment's Shermans moving up for the attack east of Caen. Author on left.

I think it was on 9 September that we sailed again for Arromanches, where it was now all peace and bustle. We immediately set off on the long chase to catch up with our advancing forces. Our vehicles all came on transporters very much covered up from public view. On reaching Belgium we halted and on finding a secret hideout started training.

From now on, except for the Rhine crossing, we operated as individual squadrons on one or two smaller projects. In October A Squadron was sent to Ostend with the object of doing some deep sea launching and navigating to a beach. This was in preparation for a possible assault with the Commandos on the island of Walcheren at the mouth of the Schelde. Before we could start any training the beach had to be cleared of booby traps left by the Germans. They were so extensive that it took the REs almost a week to clear about 200 yards. Once this was done we loaded our tanks onto the LTCs and the navy took us out to sea. At a pre-arranged spot we launched our tanks. Each tank commander stood on the top of his turret and steered with a long tiller, controlling his crew through the intercom. It was already blowing quite hard and you had to be very careful just to ease your tank off the end of the ramp or you could easily go straight to the bottom. All tanks got off safely and we set off for the shore. It was now blowing so hard and the waves were so high that I could never see all the tanks at any one time. The navigation went OK but the danger came on touch down. Our tanks drew 9 feet of water and on touch down you had to disengage the propellers, engage the tracks and dash inshore before the next wave came over the back and swamped you. Two tanks were lost and one man was drowned. As the weather continued to deteriorate the whole operation was abandoned. We returned to the regiment and continued our training on the Meuse. It was about this time that Mike Farquhar relinquished command and moved on. He was replaced as CO by John Trotter of the Guards. He was a younger brother of George who was second in command of the 2nd Fife and Forfar, and the officer who went sick on the course.

In December we went into winter quarters at Sluiskil in Zeeland. Here there was a large chemical factory with many large buildings which made good workshops. The small village was entirely dependent on the factory which was at that time out of action. The manager of the factory, with his wife, lived in a small house right in the middle of the factory complex and what a brave pair they were. The factory had been damaged by Allied bombing, but the Germans urgently wanted the production from it for their war effort. The manager worked hard to repair it, but at the same time he was a member of the Resistance movement. He had a radio fixed under his desk and interconnected to his telephone; the cross-over switch he could operate with his knee. If a German came in when he was on the radio he just moved his knee, spoke a few words in Dutch and put the telephone down. Every time the factory was just about to start production he sent a radio signal and the RAF appeared with another bomb. He and his wife never moved out of their house even when they knew a raid was coming as that would have given the thing away. We were all billeted in requisitioned houses in the village, and I got to know a Mrs Marvin who was another very brave person. Her husband had been in the French navy and was called up at the beginning of the war so she was stuck in France. She had three children aged about ten, eight and six. She housed Allied airmen until escape plans could be made for them. I made great friends with the family and all the children came and stayed with us after the war.

When Christmas came we organised a sports day for the village children with our chocolate ration as prizes; they had not seen chocolate for years. One of our officers had got a supply of brandy so we invited the parents for a drink when they came to collect their children, In some cases I think it was the children who took the parents home.

I think it was in February that we moved out of our winter quarters and started training again. About the end of the month I received a letter from Ursula telling me of the arrival of our second daughter. There followed rapid correspondence on what she should be called, all very difficult at such long range; however, we finally settled on Catriona Jane.

We had moved up to the Meuse where we had some terrific rain which interfered with our training on the river. By 23 March we were in our concentration area for the assault on the Rhine. We were to cross with the 51st Highland division commanded by Tom Rennie, whose wedding to Hulda Walker I had attended. The actual crossing went well for my squadron, but I am afraid we had quite a few casualties that day. Towards evening Tom Rennie came down the road in a Jeep and asked me to join him at his Order Group in about half an hour's time. By the time I got there he was dead, killed by a shell.

We battled on for some days against reducing opposition before we were relieved. Our swimming ability by now was very doubtful owing to damage to our canvas screens. Enough new tanks arrived to equip one squadron plus one troop and A squadron got the job of supporting the crossing of the Elbe. It took place in the end of April and we all got across with little difficulty but in the fighting that followed Squadron Sergeant Major Welsh was killed. This distressed me very much as he had not only fought all through the desert but had been my SSM ever since I joined the Regiment over a year before.

Very soon the REs had a bridge over the river and we were relieved. Most of the squadron had come back over the bridge and I was standing on it with a Military Policeman waiting for the stragglers to arrive when I witnessed a very amusing scene. Great bunches of German prisoners came trotting down the road then, during a pause, a civilian car approached. The MP stopped it. Inside was some sort of German general accompanied by two ladies in fur coats. Sitting on the side of the bridge there were two RAF chaps trying to catch up with their unit in the rush to take over installations before the Russians did. They had been on leave and had hitch hiked lifts so far but were now stuck. The MP indicated to the General with the point of his Sten gun to get out of the car. This he did and the two ladies were extracted in the same way. He then made the General open the boot and remove several suitcases. So far not a word had been spoken but now he called to the two RAF chaps, 'Here's a car for you!' At that moment my last straggler arrived and I left the General and his ladies to the MP.

When A Squadron left for the Elbe we had been billeted in a farm from which all civilians had been removed, the other squadrons being in similar positions. We all looked after the livestock in our respective farms and A squadron, having a butcher in our ranks, enjoyed some fresh pork. Another squadron promised to care for my animals while I was away but on my return I discovered that there had been a fire and all were lost.

By this time hostilities were over. We moved several times before settling down in a small town whose name I have forgotten. While there, Staff Sergeant Wilkinson, my senior fitter, got engaged to a Russian girl who had been doing forced labour for the Germans. He went and saw the Padre who said he was prepared to marry them in the local church, so a military wedding with guards of honour was laid on. I was asked if I would give the bride away. A horse-drawn carriage was produced and we drove through the town to the church. There can have been few more cosmopolitan weddings.

Life alternated between training for civilian life and sport. I was lucky and found a very nice well trained horse which gave me much fun and exercise. Demobilisation for TA soldiers was by age and my date arrived in September. After a delightful farewell dinner in Hamburg, I travelled to Redford Barracks, Edinburgh, where I was issued with my civvie jacket and trousers.

# CHAPTER 17

# Post-war readjustment

On returning home I decided I required a short holiday before resuming my civilian occupation. As the stalking season was not finished Struy was the obvious place, so Ursula and our three children, Sarah aged eight, Ian seven and Catriona eight months, all piled into the Ford Utility and off we went. The highlight of the visit was the day on the hill. The wind was in the east so with Donnie McGillivary we all piled into the Ford and drove to Deannie. We parked the car in a position from which you could see the face of Carn-a-Bahn; we left Ursula and Catriona there and the rest of us took to the hill. Sarah and Ian were good walkers and with very little help we were soon well up the hill. We spied a stag not too high up and we began our stalk. We got in fairly easily and fortunately did not have to wait and I was able to get my shot. After the gralloch we had our lunch. It was a lovely day and we were all enjoying ourselves. After lunch Donnie set off to drag the stag straight down to the road while we returned to the car.

On returning to Balgeddie the first thing was to get the Bentley off its blocks and on the road again. This enabled me to get to Kirkcaldy leaving the Ford for Ursula; I think I must have got an additional issue of petrol coupons. The staff in the house consisted of a couple, Mr and Mrs Fraser. They were a very nice pair; he worked in the garden and she helped Ursula in the house. They lived in the servants' quarters with their son Bill who was an electrician. We also had a nanny and a governess to teach Sarah and Ian.

Life soon began to get rather hectic not only in the factory but on the estate and the community and this led to my taking two decisions which I later regretted. The first was to turn down the offer of the command of the Fife and Forfar Yeo., and the second was to allow my membership of the Royal and Ancient Golf Club to lapse. After about six years I was able to rejoin the R & A but it meant restarting my membership. The other decision I could do nothing to rectify. I did however agree to join the local Home Guard which I commanded until it was disbanded.

During the war poor old Bandmaster had to go but Battlelight joined father's brood mares at Leslie home farm and produced several foals. The first of these was now old enough to be handled and fortunately Hodgson returned and we opened up our stable again at Balgeddie. Battlelight had five foals in all, Spotlight, Solomon's Son, Pilot Light, Lightheart, and Hallboy. Spotlight won the lightweight race at Fife in 1949 and Solomon's Son was second in the heavyweight race. Spotlight unfortunately died and I sold Solomon's Son as he was unnecessarily big for me and I had Pilot Light available. She won twice ridden by Michael Allenby, but much the most successful was Hallboy who won not only at Fife but one or two open races at other meetings.

I was ordained an Elder of the Kirk at Christ's Kirk on the Green, Leslie, in October 1946.

On 23 January 1947 Angus was born, and we then had our two pairs, Sarah and Ian, and Catriona and Angus after the war.

I can't remember if it was before or after Angus was born that Ian started his prep. school career at Craigflower, and it was just about this time that Miss Green replaced the other governess. She was a charming elderly lady and suggested that it would be a good idea for Sarah to have a companion once Ian went to school, suggesting a girl whom she knew called Diana Ballantyne. She turned out to be a very nice girl indeed.

About this time, Ursula's old governess Miss Leeper came to stay. The two governesses got on famously together and rarely stopped talking. One afternoon the huntsman arrived with two little fox-hound puppies for us to walk. It was a lovely afternoon and every-one assembled outside the front door and of course made a great fuss of the little puppies. Suddenly one of the old ladies turned to Will Hanley and said, 'And what are their names?' Will put his hand into his pocket and took out a postcard and read out, 'Gossip and Governess.' Will did not see the joke but the old ladies did.

In the summer of 1948 we had a super holiday in Norway. We took the Bentley and sailed from Newcastle. This was only possible as the Norwegians were offering special petrol rations to tourists. We motored about a thousand miles on very bad roads which had not been repaired during the war. The weather was perfect with temperatures in the eighties and the reception quite wonderful.

Very soon after the war the Labour Party, having nationalised the coal industry, decided to sink a new pit near Thornton to be known as the Rothes Pit. They decided that the new housing required for the miners would not be built at Thornton, but that a new town would be built to accommodate other industries as well. The area selected included the whole of the Leslie estate, parts of Balbirnie and one or two other little bits. It was obvious that there would be no future for Father to continue living in Leslie House, and this applied to a lesser extent to us at Balgeddie. The new town was to be called Glenrothes. Father was quite determined that Glenrothes should not gain possession of Leslie House so he gifted it, with the immediate grounds, to the Church of Scotland as an Eventide Home.

Just at this time Giles Walker, who had been living at Over Rankeilour since the early 1920s, died and it came on the market. Father bought it, thereby joining up the two estates of Rankeilour and Over Rankeilour. If only Over Rankeilour had come on the market instead of Leslie in 1919 what a difference it would have made.

The compensation terms under the Labour act were most punitive and I was very sorry for Father who was then over sixty-five. The new pit was a failure and enormous sums were spent attracting other industries to justify the new town.

I think it was in 1949 that I was sent to Congoleum Nairn to learn of all the new developments produced during the war which might be beneficial to us at home. Ursula came with me and we flew in an old DC4. These planes were not pressurised so we could not fly above 10,000 feet and so avoid bad weather. We seemed to spend most of the time down near sea level trying to avoid storms. We flew from Prestwick to Iceland; Gander, Newfoundland; and then to Boston where, to avoid immigration, those of us who were going on to New York were locked in a wire cage while the plane was refuelled. There were no facilities in the cage and it looked as if it was more suited to animals than to humans. All Americans thought that we had been so starved during the war that we needed feeding up, and we were grossly over-fed all the time.

Frank was of course already working with Congoleum Nairn and I think it was on this trip that he and I, along with Ursula and two engineers, were sitting in a large bar in a hotel in Baltimore. There was a group of young Americans sitting not too far away who appeared to be taking a lively interest in us. Finally, one of them came over and said to Frank and me, 'Pardon me, but I wonder if you could settle an argument for us.'

'Well, what's the problem?' we replied.

He then said, 'Are you two the acrobatic twins who are on in town tonight?'

We had to admit that we were not.

In January 1951 it was decided that I should visit Australia, but I was not keen to go by sea as George had done a couple of years earlier as it took too long, so I decided to go by air. I was at London airport waiting to board my plane when I was approached by a very pleasant young man who explained that he was from the British Red Cross. He said to me, 'Are you travelling alone and if so are you going to Singapore or beyond?'

I replied that I was alone and was going to Australia.

'I would be most grateful if you would help me because we have a lady whose son has been badly wounded in Malaya and we are sending her out to Singapore to see him in hospital.' He explained that she came from Birmingham and had never been beyond Blackpool, and would I be very kind and look after her during the flight and hand her over to the Red Cross at Singapore.

What else could I do but say, 'Yes,' so I was introduced to her and we started our journey together. In those early days we seemed to have most of our meals on the ground and we stopped off every night. We flew first to Rome where we were taken on a bus trip round the city and then given lunch at which we were each presented with a miniature bottle of Chianti. We then took off for Cairo. In flight, unbeknown to me, my charge drank her Chianti and was then violently sick.

It was dark when we landed and we were taken by bus to a large hotel for the night. The hotel hall was brilliantly lit and was full of page boys and porters all in different colourful uniforms, a sight quite new to my companion's eyes. We were shown to our rooms and hers was just across the passage from mine. At the end of the passage there sat a large fat Egyptian whose duty was to answer the bells. After a good dinner we went up to bed and as I said, 'Good night,' she said to me, 'I don't like the look of that man at the end of the passage; do you think I will be all right?' I assured her and retired to bed. As breakfast time approached next morning she knocked on my door and announced that she had not slept a wink, thinking of the man at the end of the passage. That day we lunched somewhere in Saudia Arabia and spent the night at Karachi. The next day was Delhi to Calcutta for the night, and finally, on the fourth day, we arrived at Singapore where I was relieved to hand over my charge. The fifth day we lunched in Jakarta and spent the night at Darwin, and on the sixth day we arrived in Sydney.

I must digress for a moment. Soon after the First World War my Aunt Dorothy, my father's youngest sister, married an Australian called Bruce Thomas. He would have liked to have returned to

Australia, but Aunt Dorothy said not until after her mother had died. My grandmother was in her eighties at that time but did not die until she was ninety-five, by which time the Second World War was imminent and Aunt Dorothy had two children at school. The war was now over so Aunt Dorothy agreed to emigrate with her whole family. David was married by this time but Jocelyn was not. Soon after I arrived in Sydney the Thomases arrived by sea and I met them.

After a short time they found a suitable station called Eurigar near Casino in northern New South Wales. I made many visits to them there in future years.

After a somewhat hectic time grappling with some management problems and visits to customers, in February I flew on to Wellington by flying boat from Rose Bay. On arrival I was met by Gabriel Young, our New Zealand agent. The next day we spent at Government departments trying to sort out import controls, after which we visited customers before boarding the night train for Auckland.

After the usual round of visits to customers I set off for home via the United States. Our first hop was to Nandi, Fiji, where we spent the night in some rather romantic straw huts. During this leg I was approached by one of four sunburnt young men, who came and said, 'Your name is not Nairn by any chance?'

'Yes,' I said, 'but why do you ask?'

'Well,' he said, 'it's like this. We are Rhodesians and we have been over in Australia selling tobacco. One of our suppliers in Rhodesia is called Nairn and he looks kind of like you.'

It turned out that they bought tobacco from Douglas. I never thought that I looked that much like him. From Fiji we made a fuelling stop at Canton Island before flying on to Honolulu. Owing to engine trouble we had a twenty-four-hour stopover here and I was very glad for the rest. I was put in a room with a charming young Australian. We got chatting and I said to him, 'I expect you play tennis, or something, like most of your countrymen.'

He replied, 'I do play tennis a bit.'

After a while, I discovered that he was Frank Sedgman, the then reigning World Champion who had just turned professional and was on his way to play exhibition matches in America. We had a good laugh. We then flew on to San Francisco where I changed planes and flew on via Vancouver and Calgary to Montreal. From here I flew direct to Prestwick where I landed about 19 March.

As I and my two brothers had all been at Shrewsbury School I wrote to the school, during the war, asking them to enter Ian's name for the appropriate date. When Ian was about twelve I wrote to confirm that they were holding a place for him and to finalise his exact date of entry. They replied that they had no trace of my letter and that they had no places. I sent them the carbon copy of my original letter but they refused to help unless Ian could gain a scholarship.

Ian, like his father, was no scholar; in fact he was having a struggle to make Common Entrance level. We managed to find a place at Fettes for him if he could pass the CE, and we took him away from Craigflower and sent him to a crammer at Ballachulish. He was most unhappy there as he was used as a domestic servant, so we moved him to another at Aspatria in Cumberland and he managed to get his place at Fettes where he was very happy. While there he met up with Rogie Leith, the younger son of Dick Leith who had been an officer in my squadron in the Fife and Forfar.

In 1952 Ursula and I took part in an evangelical campaign in Kirkcaldy run by the Rev. D. P. Thomson, the evangelist of the Church of Scotland. I also joined a group called the Scottish Christian Industrial Order (SCIO) and began to get more and more involved in other church work.

I am afraid that my story is not in true chronological order but more a record of incidents as they come into my mind. This little one occurred in the late 1940s. I received a cable from Frank to book a telephone call to him in New York. It so happened that we had planned to be at Struy with my parents at that time and Struy

Lodge had no telephone. I did not know what to do as I did not wish to cancel our visit as that would worry my mother, so up we went. Shortly after our arrival I went down to the telephone kiosk in the village which was the only telephone in Struy. I asked Mrs West who operated the local exchange to put me through to Inverness as I thought my problem was beyond her. I asked the operator in Inverness to book me a call to New York.

'Oh, I can't do that,' he replied, 'I shall have to put you through to London.'

When I asked the London operator to book me my call he said, 'Where are you speaking from?'

'Struy 1,' I replied.

'That can't be right,' he said, so I explained my predicament. He then said that it was impossible to book an overseas call from a call box as there was no way you could pay for it. I explained that the local post office was just beside the kiosk and could he arrange for me to pay the postmistress.

'Let me speak to her,' he said, so I shot out to look for Mrs Gordon. She wasn't there but Huie, her husband was. I persuaded him to come to the telephone and I overheard the following:

'Hallo, is that the postmistress?'

'No, she is away to Inverness for her shopping.'

'Well, who is that?'

'I'm Mr Gordon.'

'Well, are you prepared to be responsible for the payment for this call?'

'Say yes,' I prompted, so finally we got it fixed up and the call was booked for 7.30 the next morning. I had not told my mother anything as I knew she would imagine the worst. At dinner that night Germain, the butler, came into the room and announced in a loud voice: 'Mr Alastair's call to New York will come through at 7.15 and not 7.30,' so all my efforts at a cover-up were of no avail. I got my call and the matter was only a business matter and in no way a worry to my mother.

I have avoided getting involved in the details of my business life which may have given the impression that I was rarely in Kirkcaldy, but I can assure you that was far from the position. Life in Kirkcaldy was really quite hectic. Apart from all the normal problems of running a large industrial company there was a great deal of development and research, particularly into vinyl flooring. Government restrictions were legion and raw materials in short supply, all of which meant masses of meetings with government departments. Sometimes however these problems led to interesting trips. One such was an approach from a company in Johannesburg asking us to join them in setting up a vinyl tile plant there.

I got the job of going out to investigate and took Ursula with me. Naturally I notified our agent Mr Clayton and planned to visit as many customers as possible. We were asked out to dinner by a Mr Anderson of the Transvaal Rubber Company and during the evening discovered that he and I had been born in the same house in Cupar within months of one another. Mr Clayton, who was a keen wild animal man, suggested that we took two days off and visited the Kruger National Park; we readily agreed particularly as he offered to drive us there and round the park. We had a wonderful time and saw masses of wild life. Next we flew to Salisbury to see customers and spent the weekend at Villa Franca, Douglas' house. He was not there, having returned to the UK, but his manager looked after us very well. The tile venture did not materialise.

In the summer of 1949 Sarah, aged twelve, set off on a great venture: she flew to America on her own. This trip was made in response to a plea from my brother Frank. He had just been divorced and his only child Sue, also aged twelve, was staying with him being looked after by a delightful woman called Maggie. Frank thought that it would be a great help to Sue if her cousin could join her for part of the summer holidays. Sarah seemed quite happy to be travelling alone. We took her to Prestwick and she flew via Iceland and Newfoundland to New York where Frank met her. She enjoyed her American holiday and returned the same way. She went to Priorsfield School the following May.

1953 was a very busy year. Glenrothes was slowly taking more and more of Leslie, and Father got possession of Over Rankeilour. Fairly extensive alteration and redecoration was required, the chief of which were the conversion of the billiard room into a kitchen and the making of two flats out of the old domestic quarters at the back. The supervision of this fell to me. In the autumn Catriona and Angus were involved in the wedding of my niece Mary to Andrew Houston, after which I had to make a quick trip out to Australia.

The spring of 1954 saw the handover of Leslie House to the Church of Scotland well advanced and the alterations to Over Rankeilour nearing completion. We thought that it would be less of an upset for my parents if they went on one of their cruises and while they were away we organised the pack-up at Leslie and transfer to Over Rankeilour. This plan worked well and they left one home and returned to the other with everything in working order.

Before I go on to describe two rather special holidays I must record that Sarah left school in July that year, 1954. The first of the two holidays took place, I think, in 1950 and was a joint holiday with the Harrisons and the Haslops, and was to Brittany. We took Sarah and Ian but left the two little ones at home. We went in the new Bentley saloon; I had sold the old one as it was a hopeless family car. We were booked on the car air ferry which flew from Lympne to Le Touquet and while waiting for it who should come off it but Ursula's cousin Peggy Wrey and her husband Dennis. We stopped *en route* to inspect the battlefields around Caen and then went on to Morgat. Each family was a party of four. Mike and Sheila Harrison had Juliet and Hugh, Jack and Cynthia Haslop had Elizabeth and her sister, and finally there were us with Sarah and Ian. We had a very enjoyable time and returned the same way that we had come.

The second holiday was in 1954 and was to Rosapenna in

Lympne en route for Morgat.

Co. Donegal in Ireland. We calculated that, with the crossing from Stranraer to Larne, we could not make the journey in one day so we booked into a hotel in Belfast for the Friday night. It happened that I had a splitting headache when we started and Ursula drove down to Stranraer. As we were waiting to go on the boat we noticed several cars with GB plates and suddenly realised that we should have had some but we had forgotten to get them. It was Bank Holiday weekend and by the time we got to Belfast everything was closed. Saturday morning was spent in a hectic rush round to the AA and various Government offices and in the end we got the necessary documentation and GB plates and off we set for Donegal.

The hotel was wooden and our bedrooms very adequate. There was quite a large lounge and dining-room. We soon met up with another Scottish family, Gerald and June Osborne, who had two or three children about Catriona's age and younger. Ursula and June used to take it in turn to stay at home and look after the smaller ones. For the bigger ones there was a golf course, a tennis court and of course the beach.

There was a notice at the desk which said, 'Fishing permits available at the desk'. I thought that this might be fun so I applied and got my permit and a hired rod etc. Next morning Ursula said she would drop off Ian, Catriona and myself and that she and Sarah were going off somewhere else. We were dropped off at what we were convinced was the right place and off went Ursula shouting, 'We will be back about 4.30 for you.' After a short walk we found the river and started to prepare our equipment. Before we had even started fishing, a gillie appeared and asked what we were doing fishing there, so I showed him our permit.

'This is private water; you will have to go back to the hotel and check where you should have been.'

We packed up and wandered back to the road, wondering how we were going to spend the day till 4.30. We had not been at the roadside long when a little Mini drove up in which were two very fat priests. 'Like a lift?' they said, so we squeezed into the back and got a lift home.

That evening another guest came up to me and said, 'I understand you are interested in fishing: my pal is not coming till tomorrow night; would you like to take his rod for tomorrow?'

'Yes,' I said and that was arranged.

When the next day came we drove out to the very same place from which we were turned off the day before and I was introduced to the same gillie who had turned us off. We did not catch any fish.

In the autumn Sarah went to finishing school at Paddock Wood in Surrey.

It must have been about this time that we got very much involved in the Pony Club as Catriona was madly keen and had that wonderful pony Pickles. She used to go to summer camp at Perth racecourse stables where they may have been taught to groom their pony and clean their tack, but they certainly did not learn to clean themselves. Poor Angus was allergic to horses and suffered from

Golden wedding of my parents, 1956.

hayfever and other chesty problems. Because of these problems we decided to send him to Ardreck which we thought would be a helpful environment for him and it proved to be so.

In 1956 my parents celebrated their golden wedding and we had quite a large family gathering at Over Rankeilour. Also in 1956 Angus went to Ardreck, Catriona went to Priorsfield and Ian left Fettes and was called up for military service. He went first to Carlisle where he found in his batch the Master of Lovat. After Carlisle I think he spent two turns at Mons before getting his commission to the Royals. He joined his regiment in Germany along with a very, very old Ford Anglia. I must record here that Ian never touched alcohol or cigarettes, not even in the officers' mess. Sarah, having been finished, went to a Nursery Training School in Edinburgh. At the school there were several babies waiting for adoption and each one was allotted to a specific student. Sarah was allotted a half-Pakistani child. Sarah got very fond of this little boy and often took him out with her. On one occasion, Sarah arranged to meet her mother at Turnhouse where she was meeting Catriona who was being sent home from school with a threatened appendicitis. Catriona appeared with a strange woman who had taken compassion on this little twelve-year-old travelling alone and not feeling well. Ursula thanked the lady for looking after Catriona and then said, 'This is my elder daughter,' who was standing there with her little dusky baby. The woman took one look at Sarah, put her hands to her mouth and with a loud, 'Oh!' rapidly faded away. It just shows that one should not jump to conclusions.

Having finished her training Sarah started looking for a job. She heard of one in America which required an interview in London. Ursula went down with her and her prospective employer turned out to be the overseas director of Pepsi-Cola International. She got the job and on 3 February 1958 left for the USA.

The Schaeffers lived outside New York on the north side. There were two young children and Sarah had not been there very long before a third one arrived which she had to take over a few days after birth. Sarah was expected to help in the shopping and general running of the house. On one occasion the mother took Sarah and the children down to see her own mother who lived somewhere just south of New York. After some months her employers suddenly announced that they were leaving on a business trip to South America and would Sarah please look after the children and the house while they were away, so Sarah was left with the house to run and three children. I believe that on at least one occasion Sarah had to drive all her charges down to see Granny. I think Sarah stayed about eighteen months with them and got very fond of the little boy who I think was called Hal. She kept in touch with the family for a long time.

On 30 September 1958 Ursula and I set out on one of my longest and most arduous trips. We flew first to Montreal for meetings with the DOC then on to New York for meetings with Congoleum-Nairn. When in New York Sarah got time off to come and see us, which was very nice. From New York we flew via San Francisco, Honolulu and Fiji to Auckland. After a day or two there we flew on to Wellington for another couple of days, then on to Christchurch. We flew direct from Christchurch to Sydney.

I had to spend some time in Sydney with factory problems but we managed to fit in a visit to Aunt Dorothy and Uncle Bruce at Eurigar on 7 November. I think it was on this trip that we first met Jocelyn's fairly new husband Athol Robertson.

One afternoon Uncle Bruce took us out into the bush in the car to see the cattle and kangaroos. Suddenly he said, 'We must get home; there is a storm coming.' How he knew I don't know, but off we set at full speed. We just failed to make it before the storm struck. By the time we got back there was a full gale blowing and as all the house was open it was tearing through it. In Uncle Bruce's study there were newspapers blowing all over the place. We soon had the place battened down but by then the electric power had failed. Suddenly the wind stopped but there followed the most spectacular electric storm and we spent the evening watching the lightning which lit up the whole place, but there had been no rain.

David and Betty had an adjoining farm and lived with their two daughters only about half a mile away. Jocelyn with her husband Athol Robertson lived at Old Banaldo about forty miles away. They came down to show us their new baby.

After this very pleasant interlude we started a hectic round of business visits. We started in Brisbane, then went back to Sydney, down to Melbourne, over to Hobart and back to Sydney. I think it was while we were at Melbourne that we made our first visit to the Weatherlys' at Woolengoon, Mortlake. From Sydney we crossed to Perth, finally leaving there for South Africa on 17 November.

We flew by Qantas in a Super Constellation and our first leg was to the Cocas Islands. These islands were owned by a Mr Ross. There is a main island where he and most of the population lived and several smaller ones on one of which is located the aerodrome which is Australian Air Force operated. We arrived about dusk and were told that if we did not get away by ten we would have to spend twenty-four hours there. I think the explanation was that we required to navigate by the stars as there were no weather ships from which to get a fix, and also that we had to land in Mauritius in daylight.

We did not get away so had our twenty-four-hour stop-over. We were accommodated in wooden huts with eight foot high partitions, which prevented visual contact but not sound. It was very hot and we were taken out to a beach for a swim. One silly man sat too long in the sun and got very burnt. A kind lady treated him with eau-de-cologne after which he was in real agony.

After lots of food and Australian beer we took off on schedule next evening. On landing at Mauritius we had a puncture which caused a further delay as no jack could be found. Eventually they found a wedged shaped block which was placed in front of the sound twin wheel; the plane was then started up and driven up onto the block thereby lifting the punctured wheel off the ground. While waiting for all this to happen we had a chat with the captain. It was obvious from his tongue that he had some connection with Scotland so we quizzed him on where he came from.

'I was born in Scotland,' he said.

'We come from Scotland, whereabouts did you live?'

'I don't suppose you will have heard of it, a little place called Newport in Fife.'

After a short bus trip round the town and lunch we took off for Johannesburg. After a few days there we flew down to Cape Town and stayed in the Mount Nelson Hotel.

Before we started on this trip we had planned to spend Christmas in Cape Town and to have Catriona and Angus flown out. My brother Douglas, who was then living in London, agreed to put them on the plane. About three weeks before departure date, measles broke out in Catriona's school and she was sent home to stay with her grandparents at Over Rankeilour. Of course she came out with it almost next day but got over it in time to travel. Somewhere on our trip we got a letter from Ian who said he could get leave over Christmas and if we would pay for his ticket he could bring his young sister and brother out, so this was agreed. All was then ready for their arrival in Johannesburg on 19 December.

We mentioned this plan to our agent and asked him if he could help us to find somewhere more suitable to stay with the children than the Mount Nelson.

In no time at all he said he had the answer. He had a friend who had a small house overlooking the beach at Fourth Beach, Clifton, who was going to be away over Christmas and was looking for someone to look after his house while he was away; he did not even wish to be paid for it.

It was planned that we should visit Durban on our way up to collect the children. We were to fly up one evening and I got the most awful attack of hiccups. By the time we got to our hotel I was still hiccuping and was quite exhausted. I asked the hall porter if there was a chemist's shop open. 'No,' he said, 'but I know where you might get something; it stays open all night to service the hospital. I will send someone with you,' so off we set.

It turned out to be a little laboratory up a stair. I hardly had to explain my problem. He gave me three pills, with strict instructions to get into bed before taking them. I did as I was told and went out like a light; and in the morning I was cured. We flew on to Johannesburg to meet the children and when Ian came out of the plane, all 6 ft. 2 ins. of him, he was surrounded by young children. He had collected several additional charges at London Airport.

The owners of our temporary home were most trusting; they had put absolutely nothing away, not even the brushes on the dressing table. There was a black girl who went with the place who lived in a hut at the bottom of the garden.

We had a wonderful holiday. We played tennis before breakfast, swam in the rather cold sea and watched the water-ski race round Robin Island. We hired a car and drove down to the Cape of Good Hope, went up to the top of Table Mountain, visited the vineyards and even went to a drive-in cinema. We returned home refreshed and sunburnt.

There is one other journey which I think I ought to record which took place in the early fifties. I had been breaking Hallboy and took a liberty with him and landed up with a broken heel. Ian Patterson operated on it and I was in hospital for some time before emerging with my leg in plaster. Ian informed me that I would have to remain in plaster for four months. Now, I was due to go to a meeting at Congoleum-Nairn so I asked Ian if I could go in plaster.

He said, 'Oh, yes, but I shall put a strong walking iron on and a new plaster.'

I went into the hospital, pulled up my trouser leg and the deed was done. When I got home that evening I discovered that there was no way I could get my trousers over this new walking iron. Ursula had the brilliant idea of opening up the side seam of my trousers and inserting a zip.

We planned to travel by sea and booked on the *Medea*, a 19,000 ton first class only Cunarder. I had applied to the exchange control for extra dollars for Ursula to come to look after me and got them. We sailed from Liverpool and as soon as we left the river, ran into a gale. The sea got rougher and rougher and although the ship was fitted with stabilisers we pitched violently. Ursula took her sea-sick

The family at Struy, 1956. Self, Sarah, Ursula, Ian Catriona, Shadow (Irish wolf hound), Angus.

pills but still felt terrible although not sick. The doctor invited us to a drinks party and we went. By this time Ursula was complaining of double vision and when she failed to pick up a glass the doctor agreed that there was something far wrong and sent her to bed with a different pill. In the cabin she said she must have air and persuaded me, against my better judgement, to open the port hole. Within minutes solid green water was pouring in.

I spent quite long periods up forward watching the huge waves coming over the bows and rushing out of the sides. Eventually we arrived in New York about two days late. The rest of the trip went well and I found a 'stukey leg' a great help in getting across the New York streets.

In the early 1950s Father was struck another blow. He was struggling with the problems of Glenrothes and the move from Leslie when the North of Scotland Hydro-Electric Board announced that they wished to build a scheme in Glen Strathfarrar. Father and Shemi Lovat (Lord Lovat) agreed that they would jointly oppose it at the public enquiry. They appointed a QC and various experts to prepare their case; then suddenly we read in the paper: 'Lord Lovat comes to terms with Hydro Board,' without a word to Father. As Lovat was by far the largest land-owner this ruined Father's case. The compensation terms for damage to the fishing were most unfair. They were based on the average number of fish caught over, I think, the last five years. Lovat's fishings had been commercially let over that period and reflected their true value, but Father had only fished with my mother and a few guests and their catch in no way reflected the commercial value of the Struy fishings. The Scheme started in 1957. The consultants were Halcrow and Partners and the builders Mitchell Construction Company. During 1958 and 59 most of the work was preparatory work such as setting out datum lines, putting up huts and, most important, rebuilding the glen road so that it could carry the extra traffic.

# CHAPTER 18

# That fateful year

I think I should put on record something about the Meldrum family. About the mid-thirties Father was looking for a keeper for Leslie. He had an application from one George Meldrum from Kinaldy. It was arranged for him to come to the estate office in Kirkcaldy and I was present at that interview. When the poor man came in he looked like a thug, with one eye completely closed and swollen. He had in fact been stung by a wasp. The interview went well however, and he was offered the job which he accepted. Meldrum was a few months older than me and was already married. He took up residence in the keeper's house at Leslie with one little son, Billy, and he continued to live there until he moved to Rankeilour about 1960. It wasn't long before a second son, Ian, was born, and these two boys were just older than our Sarah and Ian. Shortly after the birth of Ian Mrs Meldrum developed rheumatoid arthritis and was crippled with it for the rest of her life. Meldrum was a great help to Ursula during the war in many ways and he and our Ian became very good friends.

After the war Meldrum began taking an interest in gun-dog field trials. Soon success began to come his way and he made a lot of friends in that community. This in its turn led to invitations to pick up at some of the larger shoots, one of which I think was at Drumkilbo. It so happened that the Queen used to be present at the latter and as she was interested in gun-dog trials she made herself known to Meldrum and they had several chats on the subject.

Billy Meldrum, after leaving school, had health problems for a year or two but by the time he was twenty he was back in the keepering world and used to accompany his father to the trials and on occasions got an opportunity to run one of his dogs. About 1959 he married my mother's table-maid, Annie. Shortly after, an invitation, or possibly I should call it a summons, arrived for him to appear with his wife at Sandringham for interview as prospective dog trainer and kennelman. The Queen, the Duke of Edinburgh and the factor conducted the interview, at the end of which the Queen turned to Billy and said, 'Would you like the job?'

'I should like to think about it, Ma'am,' he replied.

'You are quite right,' she replied. 'Go home and then let me know your decision.'

Home they came and the family all arrived at Balgeddie wondering what they ought to do. Billy was worried that he might not be up to the job and that he would let the Queen down. After a short discussion it was decided that it was an opportunity not to be missed and that it was almost a Royal Command so the decision was that he should accept.

Once installed at Sandringham he was told that, after a suitable period for assessment, he was to report on all the dogs and make recommendations as to their future. Apart from one or two gun-dogs belonging to the Queen there were many other dogs belonging to other members of the Royal Family. He was keen to get rid of all these extra dogs and went to the factor's office to make his verbal report, but there he was told that the Queen wished a written report in his own hand. The answer he got was that, if he could find homes for them, he could get rid of all the extras but that none were to be put down. From that day on Billy has gone from strength to strength and he is now head keeper with at least two other keepers and a dog man under him.

Soon after Billy's move to Sandringham Meldrum moved from Leslie to Rankeilour on the retirement of his older brother Bob who was ten years his senior.

Poor Mrs Meldrum's rheumatics got progressively worse, and after operations on her knee and other treatments she became house-bound. In the meantime Meldrum was having a very successful trial career. A day came when the Queen's dog received a badly cut foot just before going to Balmoral so Billy rang his father and asked him if he had a dog that the Queen could borrow. Meldrum replied that she could have Jade but he must have her back by the end of September as she was entered in the championship trials after that. So Jade went and returned in due time. She won the championship and when the Queen heard she rang Meldrum and congratulated him and expressed relief that she had not spoiled her.

Some considerable time later Meldrum recieved a signal that the Queen would be calling at his house at a specified time. She duly arrived, driving herself and accompanied by her detective. Stepping from the car she announced, 'I have brought my dogs to see you,' and out jumped the corgis. She stopped for tea with the Meldrums before going on to Edinburgh.

After a time Meldrum himself began to suffer from arthritis and he had to have a hip replacement. By the time Meldrum got to retiral age it was becoming obvious that they could not cope on their own and they moved to Leslie House Eventide Home. They were very happy there though Mrs Meldrum did not live long, but poor Meldrum got cancer in his face which led to some very painful and disfiguring operations. I am afraid his last few years were not very happy ones.

Sarah reached her twenty-first birthday while working in America and Ian passed his while serving in Germany. In 1960 Sarah and Ian were both home; Sarah was working in London and Ian had started in the factory in Kirkcaldy. As the Leslie Estate staff had presented Ian with a fishing rod for his twenty-first we invited them to a small drinks party at Balgeddie at which Meldrum proposed Ian's health and Ian replied. In April Hallboy won the Fife members race ridden by Michael Allenby. Just at this time the

company, inspired by Sandy McIntosh, were investigating the pos-
sibility of building a chipboard plant in Inverness and Sandy wished
me to join him in Germany to investigate some possible plant
purchase. As I had to attend a European Linoleum Manufacturers
Meeting in Nice in June I planned to combine the visits. On 11 June
Ursula and I crossed to Ostend and headed for Germany.

Having completed our business there we continued over the Alps,
through north-west Italy and on to Nice. We arrived back in London on Sunday 19 June. Ursula had planned to stay a week with
her mother and that she would keep the car for her use as I planned
to come south again the next weekend, I think to go to Henley. I
took the night sleeper train to Edinburgh. When I alighted from the
train I was met on the platform by Robert and Burgess, the family
factor. I cannot describe my feelings when they informed me that
Ian had been killed, along with Rogie Leith, on Sunday afternoon,
19 June. The two boys had been at Struy for the weekend and were
returning to Balmedy to drop Rogie when on a straight stretch of
road near Old Meldrum a farmer had emerged from a farm road
and their car left the road and landed upside down, killing both
boys and Miss B, the family dog. I returned to Kirkcaldy with
Robert and Burgess and rang Ursula and then Sarah from the can-
teen. We contacted Priorsfield who thought that Catriona should
come home and then Eton, where Angus was in his first year, and
we decided to leave Angus at school. The plan was for Ursula and
Sarah to fly up that afternoon, and as Catriona's school thought that
she should return, she joined the party.

After some breakfast I borrowed the office car and set off for
Aberdeen to see the Leiths, and on with the police to identify Ian's
body. Grainger, the office driver, met the ladies at Turnhouse and
brought them back to Balgeddie. I arrived back later completely
exhausted both mentally and physically. We managed to arrange for
the funeral to be held at Kirkcaldy Crematorium on the Wednesday
and for the interment of the ashes in Momimail cemetery on
Thursday.

Life had to return to normal but I don't remember much about the next few weeks. I am sure we must have gone south and recovered the car, if nothing else.

During the summer Father's health deteriorated and he was unable to go to Struy which was a great disappointment to him. I see from my diary that I made a trip to Canada and the USA starting on 11 September, after which we had a short holiday at Struy. On return it was obvious that Father was sinking and he died early on the morning of 20 October, aged eighty. The funeral was held in the Bow Kirk on 25 October, the twenty-fifth anniversary of our wedding. A memorial service was held later in St Brysdale Church in Kirkcaldy.

All this time it was becoming clear that our time at Balgeddie was drawing to a close. We looked at various houses but could not find anything suitable. Now, on Father's death, it made it more important that we should be near Mother at Over Rankeilour. With this end in view I started to negotiate with Murray Mitchell to give up the tenancy of West Hall so that we could move in there. In the end we came to terms but he demanded his pound of flesh, and why shouldn't he? Anyway, I thought it was worth it.

The house had been occupied by a farm worker and no improvements had been made for many years. It was obvious that much would have to be done and we engaged Mr Watson of Haxtons and Watson to act as architects. Plans were then made and of course planning permission was required. All this took time and I think it must have been some time in 1963 before work started.

I must turn the clock back once again. When the war started Father had been Master of Foxhounds and he remained so throughout the war. It was largely through his efforts that the hounds survived the war. After the war, when he was already over sixty-five, he handed over to younger people. He continued to hunt for a year or so but with the move from Leslie and other pressures he finally gave up.

My stable was running smoothly with Hodgson in charge but it was not long before he was offered a considerable rise in salary by another Fife Fox Hound follower and I did not blame him for accepting. His new job did not last too long and the last I heard of Hodgson he was away from horses and working in Edinburgh. By now I had to be away from home a lot and required a reliable man to look after my horses. This I found difficult and had a number of changes and finally in the early sixties, with a pending move to West Hall, I gave up the struggle. I lent Hallboy to John Roger who had ridden him in several point-to-points. Soon after he broke a leg and had to be put down.

When Father gave up being Master he started a small herd of pedigree Aberdeen Angus cattle. I soon began to get interested and when Father moved to Over Rankeilour in 1954 I took over the herd. There were two ways to be successful in this field. The first was to be *the* farmer, to have both knowledge and an eye for a beast and move in that environment, and the other was to employ either a manager or a herdsman to do it for you. We were neither and so remained on the periphery; nevertheless we enjoyed it and the minor successes we had. This venture also ended with the move from Balgeddie.

Another ploy in which I got involved after the war was membership of the North-East Fife Hospital Board. This was before the days of the Health Boards and we were only responsible for the hospitals in Kirkcaldy and those to the east. Very soon, the building of the first phase of the new Victoria started and we foresaw that there would be a necessity for a greatly increased intake of student nurses and I was asked to head a committee to organise this. Our head nurse tutor was a Mrs Halkeston, a splendid woman in every respect. We planned to issue a brochure to be widely distributed, especially round the schools and colleges. Just at that time the first of the hospital programmes was on the television, called 'Emergency Ward 10' and was very popular. I wrote to the leading lady, explaining our problem and asking if she would agree to her photograph being on the outside of our brochure. She readily agreed and sent us several to choose from. The plan worked and the recruits flowed in. I think the young lady's name was Jill Brown and when she got married and came to Scotland for her honeymoon she called in to enquire how we were getting on. After about fifteen very enjoyable years, the health service was reorganised and Health Boards were set up; and appointments became political so I bowed out.

# CHAPTER 19

# Mostly travel

B y the time Father took possession of Over Rankeilour in 1953 farming activities at Leslie were already being eroded by the activities of Glenrothes, and Jim Simpson took over both farms.

No improvements had been made to the farm at Over Rankeilour since the dairy had been built just after the First World War. I don't remember exactly what happened to the last tenant, Tom Methven, but I know that he was old and not very fit and that he had just carried on a very limited activity and had let some of his land. It was obvious that things were run down and that if an active farming operation was to be undertaken, considerable modernisation would be necessary.

Step one was the replacement of the old open circular cattle courts and their replacement with what we considered at the time to be a very modern layout. There was a large central silage pit with four courts on either side, all under one roof. The farmhouse was also modernised at this time and Simpson moved from Leslie to Over Rankeilour.

The Government was calling for ever more production and as the land was not suited for sheep owing to a mineral defect we decided to set up a pig unit. While this was being planned, with guidance from the East of Scotland College of Agriculture, the new cattle facilities were being run in. The new pig unit consisted of a fattening unit and a farrowing unit. The dry sows were housed in the old dairy byres. At the same time a grain drier and storage unit were built so that we could be self sufficient as far as possible. The dunging passage in the fattening house was on slats and the effluent emptied into a large outside slurry pit, about 10 ft. deep, covered with roofing felt and wire netting to prevent anyone falling in. This set-up worked well but we soon found that we could put more pigs through the fattening house than the farrowing house could supply. The next step was to put up a new dry sow house and convert the old cow byre into additional farrowing. This proved to be a very profitable unit, the biggest difficulty being pig health. At our peak we were turning over about 1,200 pigs a year. After these units had been going for some time there was a great scare one morning when it was discovered that the young Charolais bull was missing. A search was started but no one had seen him. Later someone saw a little bit of felt sticking up on the slurry pit cover. There he was, standing in the bottom in about three feet of slurry. To get him out we had to take the lid off the pit, lower a cattle crate into the pit and drive him in, then, with the aid of Houston's mobile crane, lift him out. After a good hosing down he was none the worse.

Life at this time was very full. First there were all the local calls, such as the hospital board, the church and others, then there were meetings in Batley, Yorkshire, J. Williamson in Lancaster, the timber division in Inverness and innumerable visits to London for Linoleum Association meetings and Federation meetings with the trade unions. There were visits to Compagnie Français de Linoleum Nairn in Paris and of course Canada, America and Australia. In addition, just at this time there were problems arising from the hydro board activities at Struy.

Talking of Struy, it was just about this time that the last of our ponies died and we found it very difficult to hire suitable ones to get the deer off the hill so we were dragging them down. Nobody liked this job and we searched and searched for a mechanical means of getting them off the hill. One machine we tried was called a Hauflinger. It had four-wheel drive and differential locks on both axles. It could carry about six people and one or two stags. I think it would be about 1963 when we had Howson and Elizabeth and

Mike and Sheila staying; and Mike was to go stalking with Donnie
Fraser on the Culligran side. I asked the ladies if they would like
to drive up in the Hauflinger and see if we could get a stag on our
own. This was agreed and Howson, the three ladies and myself
drove up. We spotted a stag to get to which meant leaving our
vehicle and doing a detour on foot. It was a lovely warm day and
it was not long before I was carrying not only the rifle but masses
of ladies' jerseys. We eventually got round to a wonderful view spot
from which the ladies could watch the final stalk. Howson was
armed with a camera, as he doesn't rifle shoot, and he and I went
off together. All went very well and I shot my stag. After the
gralloch Howson and I dragged it a short distance to a burn and I
went to fetch the Hauflinger. I got back with no problems and after
lunch we all piled in and off we went. Everything was going fine
when I failed to notice, in an area of bog myrtle, a small ditch and
in went the two wheels on the right side. The machine slowly tipped
over onto its side spilling all the ladies, the stag and Howson and
me onto the ground. No one was hurt but what a job we had getting
it out! We had to send for help, which fortunately was not too far
off. It got bogged again another day very soon afterwards so that
was another failure.

During my earlier visits to Sydney I had tried to find persons
with a successful track record to serve as non-executive directors
on the Board of Michael Nairn (Australia) Ltd. I did find people
but I am afraid they did not have the effect I had hoped for.
However most of them became personal friends, and in particular
I must mention Harry and Gwen Hattersley. They, with their
teenaged son Richard, came to stay with us at Balgeddie in 1963.
Harry had been Australian amateur golf champion and was a member of the R & A. They had a hired car and were looking round
Scotland. One day they returned and Harry presented me with four
golf clubs which he had bought from Nicoll of Leven. 'There you
are,' he said, 'Now you can start playing golf,' and so golf replaced
horses as one of my favourite recreations. Unfortunately Harry

died quite young during one of my subsequent visits to Australia. Richard, with his charming wife Su, have become firm friends.

Another family, whom I think we got to know through their daughter Katie who was at Wingfield with Catriona were Bert and Leslie Locke. They stayed with us in Scotland and we stayed with them in Sydney. Unfortunately they too have passed on but their son Nick and Sue and family have taken their place.

In 1961 Ursula and I made another of these quick trips to Australia into which we managed to fit two week-end visits, one to Aunt Dorothy and the other to the Croppers at Willowtree. We returned via Congoleum-Nairn and the DOC. I think it was in May 1963 that we attended Robert's wedding to Joanna Salt which took us all the way to Hampshire.

When in 1963 it looked as if another visit to Australia would be necessary I thought it would be nice to take the girls and have a bit of a holiday *en route*. Sarah, now nearly twenty-seven, and Catriona aged nineteen had never had any coming-out party, so this was to take its place. Once the programme was fixed and we knew our dates in Sydney we contacted Harry Hattersley and asked him if he could find us a flat. He replied that all was fixed and that he would meet us at the airport, but he did not say where the flat was. We left London early in January 1964. It was a lovely day and we had a beautiful view of Europe before landing at Beirut. It was light when we left there but dark when we landed at Delhi about eleven o'clock.

Next day was bright but cool so we decided to walk down to the old town to see some old fort. We were informed on our return that walking with three white ladies was unusual, but we came to no harm. We hired a car the next day and drove to Agra. We stayed overnight in Laurie's Hotel as Ursula was determined to see the Taj Mahal both by daylight and by moonlight. We also visited the red fort. On the way back to Delhi we had a puncture and as we had no spare wheel we had a problem. After a long time sitting in the car in a village surrounded by little black faces with big brown eyes, our driver appeared with a wheel. So that was India and next day we flew to Bankok.

We only had two days here so we went out to a restaurant and dined sitting on the floor, and of course we ate curry. Quite early the next morning we went with a guide by boat through the floating market. The afternoon was spent visiting various pagodas and temples. The buildings were well worth seeing. We set off next day in a hired car for some place but once more we had a puncture. During the long delay we amused ourselves watching a small boy guiding a water buffalo while standing on its back.

Early the next morning we flew down to Singapore where we checked our baggage in for the flight to Perth late that night. This done we flew up to Kuala Lumpur for the day to see Waveney, Ursula's niece who had just given birth to her first-born, a boy named Mark. After the inspection Peter took us for a drive around before we flew back to Singapore.

We were standing in the queue waiting to board when I was called to the Qantas desk. I was informed that London had over-booked the plane by four and as we were a party of four we would have to wait for the next one. 'When is that?' I asked.

'In two days' time,' I was told.

I was furious as I had meetings in Perth, and demanded to see the Qantas manager. He was in town and took some time to arrive. I tore into him and told him that I had met his chairman and would make a point of having it out with him when I arrived in Sydney. He said there was nothing he could do but he drove us to the best hotel and fixed us up with rooms.

We had hardly got into bed when the manager returned and said he had got us space on a charter plane for Asian students going to Perth. Having done a quick pack up we were rushed out to the airport and placed in the first class seats on a plane full of students. On arrival at Perth the red carpet was out and we were ushered through all formalities and into the hands of John Tomlinson, our WA agent and a great friend of mine. We stayed in the Esplanade

Hotel, a fine modern building very different to the old wooden one I had stayed in in 1934. Ursula made contact with several members of the Devitt family, most of whom were either second or third generation Australians. After quite a social time and a few business calls we moved on to Sydney on 7 February.

Here we were met, as promised, by Harry Hattersley who still refused to tell us where our flat was to be. We drove right through the city and over the Harbour Bridge to the north side. We finally stopped outside 3 Kirkoswald Avenue, Harry's house. He and Gwen had moved out and were staying in his sister's house as she was away on a trip, and we were to have their house. It quite took our breath away, it was such a wonderful large house with a lovely garden and view. Anyway there we were and there we were based for the next month.

After a day or so we went up to Canberra for one night to let the girls see the capital and then on to Melbourne. Here we hired a car and drove out to Mortlake to stay a couple of days with the Weatherleys. Catriona had already met James when he was up at Trinity Hall. While there, Bill took us out in the car to some woods to see the koala bears in the wild. After a day in Melbourne visiting customers we returned to Sydney.

Ursula and the girls had quite a lot of contacts and started a round of social events in which I joined in the evenings. On 18 February Ursula, Sarah and I flew up to Eurigar for two days to see Aunt Dorothy and Uncle Bruce. Catriona stayed behind with some of her young friends. We had almost two more weeks in Sydney before leaving for Christchurch on 3 March. Here we hired a car and dashed down to Lake Hayes to see Colin and Elle Speight for two days, then back to Christchurch and over to Wellington. Here we hired another car and drove to Auckland via Rotorua.

On 20 March we were off again, this time for Nandi and Honolulu. Just before we set off on this trip Juliet Harrison had announced her engagement to a very nice American called Tuckerman Moss. We met them and when we told them of our pending trip Tuck said, 'My brother manages one of the big hotels in Honolulu; I will write and tell him you will be coming.'

As we emerged from the customs we were met by Mr and Mrs Moss and conveyed in the most enormous car to the hotel. We were only staying two nights but nevertheless we were shown into the most beautiful penthouse suite. Next evening the Mosses took us out to dinner and a floor show at another hotel quite close by. Ursula was not feeling too well so she did not come. After the show was over I was walking home with Mrs Moss when a young American couple stopped us and after introducing themselves turned to me and said, 'You wouldn't produce cattle in Scotland by any chance?'

I replied that I did have a small herd of Aberdeen Angus.

'Oh,' he said, 'I thought I recognised you; I saw your photograph in my uncle's magazine.'

It turned out that his uncle came regularly to the Perth bull sales and had received a copy of the *Aberdeen Angus Magazine*. In it there was a photograph of the sale ring and I just happened to be sitting near his uncle watching the sale.

On we went next day to New York for a quick visit to Congoleum-Nairn, then up to Montreal and home by 1 April.

While on the subject of travel I must admit to one terrible blunder I made. George and I were to go to a meeting in Paris and he said he would organise the tickets. I was handed my tickets in good time and forgot about them. Ursula wished to take the opportunity to visit her mother in London. As the meeting was to be on Monday we agreed to go to London by night sleeper on Friday and that I would fly out on Sunday evening on a different flight to George. On Saturday morning I suddenly realised that, although I had my tickets, I did not have my passport. I rang up poor Burgess at his home and asked him if he would go into the office in Kirkcaldy, pick up my passport and take it to Turnhouse and put it on a plane for London marked to be called for. This he agreed to do and I thought all was well. On Sunday Sarah came to Mrs

Devitt's flat and offered to drive me down to Heathrow. I said goodbye to her there and went in search of my passport; I was handed an envelope with what I took to be my passport inside. I then checked my baggage in and went to the emigration. Pulling my passport from its envelope I handed it to the officer. He looked at it for some time, then looked up at me and read out, 'Angus Spencer-Nairn, 4ft. 9 ins. Student. Doesn't look much like you, Sir,' he said. 'I am afraid there is nothing I can do,' and he handed me back the passport.

What was I to do? My baggage had gone and I could not get it back. I rang Burgess again and he agreed to collect the right passport, take it to Turnhouse and find the first plane it could come down on and then ring me at the hotel. This he did and I think it was due between eight and eight thirty the next morning so I booked myself on the next flight to Paris after that. After an anxious night I collected the horrid thing and caught my flight, but what a job I had finding my baggage in Paris! Although the meeting was not due to start till ten I was at least an hour late. One good lesson learnt.

The only other thing of note that I can remember in that year was Juliet and Tuck's wedding which was, I think, in May in East Anglia as Mike and Sheila were still living at Chestnut Farm at that time.

Angus left school in December 1965 and flew out to Australia in January.

February 1965 saw me off to Australia again, but this time we went via Canada where I attended the AGM of the DOC on the way. We were booked to fly early one morning to New York and pick up a Qantas plane there. The weather suddenly deteriorated, with freezing rain, and we were advised to fly out at once and book into the New York airport hotel. It was just as well we did as Darval was closed next day; however, our troubles were not over. Our plane was continually being diverted from one airport to another by fog and when it arrived over New York the same thing

happened and it was sent to Washington. There were quite a group
of us including some women with children. We were put on a bus
and told that it would take us to Washington, but by the time we
had got halfway to New York our driver said it was too foggy and
that he would drop us at Grand Central Station where we could
catch a train. At the station there was not a redcap to be seen so I
marshalled the men and we carried the luggage down to the
platform. When the train came in from Boston it stopped on a curve
which left a big gap opposite the door. As we were struggling to
get the women and children over this gap, the guard appeared and
shouted, 'Get in, I'm going.' We just managed it in time.

It was the small hours of the morning when we reached
Washington and on enquiry, we discovered that our plane was not
at the international airport but at a US Air Force base. We piled
into taxis and after quite a drive arrived. We found our plane but
as there were no civilian services no fresh supplies were available.
We had to go all the way to San Francisco before we got a meal.
Such were the joys of air travel.

We changed planes at Honolulu and flew on to Auckland and
finally on to Sydney where my main business was. Angus met us
and we all flew up to Casino for the weekend. We also saw Robert
and Joanna in Sydney as Robert was working in the office in
Auburn at the time. I also had a problem to try and sort out in
Johannesburg so we flew to Perth and on there. After a few days
there we returned to London. Angus returned to the UK in August
and started with Chiene and Tait in September.

In January 1961 my mother, accompanied by Freda, a nurse
companion, set off on a world cruise. I think the boat was called
the *Orsova* and they sailed east to Australia. It so happened that
Ursula and I were in Sydney that February and met Mother there;
Ursula thinks that we caught up with her again in Auckland.
Anyway I know she returned via the Panama Canal and New York.
I have a feeling she went on another cruise in 1963 but who she
went with I cannot remember. Somewhere along the line she had a

fairly major operation and a warning of cancer, but on 5 October 1965 she celebrated her eightieth birthday. Soon after that the cancer began to take over and she died at home on 26 January 1966, and so both my parents just made eighty, and now they were both gone. How blessed we had been with our parents, so loving and caring, never demanding, who brought us up, or should I say led us up by example.

By this time our alterations at West Hall were well advanced and we were looking forward to moving over within months. Ursula and I decided that we would move into Over Rankeilour to be in the centre of things, and try and make up our minds if we wished to stay on there or move into West Hall. Before we could do so we had to dispose of all the furniture most of which now belonged to the other members of the family. Over Rankeilour had been left to me but the furniture and other movables were to be shared within the family. I had an inventory prepared and we all gathered and in order of age selected items. After the first round the second round was started by No. 2 and so on. All went well and the house was cleared within a day or two. After some very happy months we decided that as the children were all away from home it was too big a house for just two people and that we would move down to West Hall when it was finished.

28 October saw us off to Australia again but we were home by mid December. West Hall was ready enough for us to move so we decided to try and make the move before Christmas. We made it twenty-nine years almost to the day since we moved into Balgeddie. We were sorry to leave Balgeddie, after all it was our house especially built for us, but in the end, owing to the circumstances, we were ready to go.

# CHAPTER 20

# West Hall

W e were hardly settled into West Hall before Sarah announced her engagement to John Scoular. They had known one another for some time and we were wondering if and when this might happen. Sarah was twenty-nine and John in his thirties and they did not wish a long engagement so the wedding was fixed for 28 April 1967. Sarah was not for a large wedding in Fife but just a quiet family ceremony in London. From my point of view this was just as well as I had to make another quick visit to Australia. I left on 7 March and was home again by early April. Ursula stayed at home to be available to help Sarah and spent the rest of the time visiting her family.

Sarah, true to form, decided that she was not going to be a traditional bride but was going to wear what we thought was a rather odd trouser suit. The wedding was held in the small chapel at St Columba's, Pont Street, and there were only about fourteen of us present. The wedding was in the morning and was followed by a luncheon in a hotel. As all this was so low key we laid on a cocktail party in the Cavalry Club for a wider number of guests. There was one problem, Sarah's trouser suit, as no such garment was permitted in the Cavalry Club. In the end Sarah agreed to conform and wear a dress.

In the Club that night there was another Regimental cocktail party and for some reason or other the club officials failed to keep the guests for the two parties apart. Quite a few young officers, probably from different regiments from the one hosting the party, came and shook hands with Ursula and me before realising what was wrong, and on the other side one of Ursula's aunts spent the evening at the regimental party where she met several friends.

At the height of the party Ursula called to me in one of her best stage whispers: 'It's terribly hot in here, can you do anything about it?'

Immediately a young man standing nearby sprang to the large casement window and threw up the bottom section. As he let go it crashed down and there followed a tinkling of falling glass as the panes fell into the area outside. There was a ghastly silence for a moment and a voice was heard to ask, 'Has someone fallen through the window?' The unfortunate young man had not realised that the window had no sash cords and balance weights. The party went on, now with plenty fresh air.

Early one January morning in 1968 we were woken by something knocking against the window and the sound of a mighty rushing wind. The noise of the wind was so great that you could not make out what was happening. In the morning, well before it was light, the back door bell rang. I opened it and there stood a very white-faced grieve. I could not repeat his words here but he was very frightened. The wind had slackened by this time but nevertheless a tile off his roof had just missed his head as he emerged from his house; then, before he reached the farm he could just make out part of the steading roof lying in the field. On arrival at the farm he found that the old tiled roof of the cattle court had collapsed and the cattle were all standing amongst the fallen timbers and tiles. Fortunately, none of them seemed to be any the worse. The gable end and door of the big 90 ft. by 125 ft. storage shed had fallen in and at least half of the asbestos sheets of the roof were shattered. We had several hundred tons of potatoes stored in that shed which were all covered with straw.

I was scared that they would get either soaked or frosted so I rushed to the telephone, and, believe it or not, it was working. I rang R. S. Wilson, builders in Cupar who came straight out and

there was not a single tree across the road. He promised to get
started at once, as we were first in the queue. All the other roads
round about were blocked with fallen trees. We had a number of
out-wintered cows and calves, and so many fences had been
flattened by trees that we found them scattered about all over the
place, looking for the food which we could not get to them.
Leuchars recorded gusts of 100 m.p.h. that night. It took two men
with power saws three days to clear the road between West Hall
and Over Rankeilour farms.

Later in the summer Catriona came to stay and I suggested that
we might go up to Perth and hire a plane and she could fly me
round Fife, inspecting all the damage done by the gale. This we did
with me navigating visually while she did the flying. We had a most
enjoyable and interesting afternoon. Catriona had learnt to fly some
eighteen months earlier at Biggin Hill. She had taken Ursula and
me up from Biggin Hill on a previous occasion.

Down in the office Willis Roxburgh and Brian Gilbert had now
been with us for some time and my work-load was slackening, so
in February 1968 we thought we would have a little holiday. Armed
with our golf clubs we flew to Grand Bahama to inspect our properties. Some years earlier, before the Bahamas obtained their
independence, we were recommended by a cousin of Ursula's to
invest in some building land, as things were booming there at that
time. When independence came however the bottom fell out of that
market and so our plots remained undeveloped as they have to this
day. After a lovely week playing golf we flew on to Bermuda where
Peter and June Devitt had taken a house. We played golf here too
and on one occasion Ursula sliced her drive and it landed in a
garden. She played another and we went off to retrieve the first one.
The lawn was covered in golf balls but it was not long before we
knew why. A sort of Great Dane dog appeared growling fiercely.
We retreated but the beast followed us for about a hundred yards.
This was a very good holiday.

In April Angus, who was only twenty-one and still serving his apprenticeship as a chartered accountant said that he wished to announce his engagement to Christina Gillies who was two and a half years older than he was and was a Roman Catholic. We discussed it and as he appeared to have thought it well through we raised no objection and the engagement was announced on 6 April. Tina was the elder daughter of Colonel and Mrs Gillies of New Abbey, Dumfries.

Angus had been living in digs in Royal Circus and now had to find married quarters. They found a top floor flat in Frederick Street. We had some furniture stored in Over Rankeilour for just such an occasion. The selected items were loaded into the trailer horse box and off we went to Edinburgh. It was a tough task carting everything up four flights of stairs and we were nearly beaten by the box mattress which did not wish to go round the last bend, but after a lot of pushing we made it. They were married in July in the Roman Catholic Church in Edinburgh which was much more convenient for us than New Abbey would have been.

About Christmas of that year Catriona announced her engagement to Paul Kirton. I think she first met him with Jane Anstruther-Gray. This wedding was, of course, our responsibility. She wanted to be married in the Bow Kirk and that was fine by us; the problem was where to hold the reception. It was solved by getting a contractor to erect the inside of one of his marquees inside one end of our large potato shed and putting a wooden floor over the concrete one. The wedding was held on Saturday 28 March 1969 which happened to be Grand National day. I believe the winner was called Highland Wedding. It all worked out very well except that the band leader at the dance in the evening got drunk. Now they were all married with homes of their own.

Ever since Father had died in 1960 Douglas and I with our respective families had been sharing Struy. This arrangement worked quite well but we found it difficult to dovetail our visits, so in May 1969 we decided to split the place in two. The only sensible dividing line seemed to be the river Farrar and after discussion we agreed that Douglas would take all the land north of the river and me all the land south of it. This decision has worked very well as both families get on so well together.

Unfortunately Douglas did not live long to enjoy it as he died in November 1970, some six weeks before his sixty-fourth birthday.

January 1970 saw us off to Australia again but this time we deliberately built in two one-week holidays. We flew straight to Sydney where we stayed in Bert and Lesley Locke's lovely flat. At the beginning of February we flew to Auckland to see our agent John Young, then went on to Christchurch for our first holiday period. We had been told so often that we should visit the South Island west coast so we hired a car and drove to the Franz Joseph Glacier hotel for two nights. On entering the hotel whom should we meet but Mr and Mrs Playfair-Hanny whose home at that time was Baltilly House, Ceres.

Next morning we were to be taken a guided walk up the glacier but it was pouring with rain and there was low mist. Later in the day it cleared and the guide asked if anyone wished to go for a shortened tour. There were several volunteers and off we went. All went well until we came to a rather steep part where the guide started cutting steps in the ice with his axe. Ursula decided to go no further. I scrambled up a bit further and then decided that this was not for me. At that point there was a general mix-up and the guide had a problem sorting us out.

Next day we drove on to Milford where we met another Fife couple, then on via Queenstown to Weather Hill at Ohai where we stayed with Richard and Jenny Speight for four days. I have never seen so many sheep; they were gathering for some reason and they poured down the hill in thousands.

After this happy break it was up to Christchurch and over to Melbourne. We left Sydney on 4 March for Perth to see John Tomlinson, our agent there. Finally we left Perth on 9 March for the second bit of holiday. We landed in Johannesburg early in the morning, changed planes, and flew to Durban to join Peter and June at their holiday hotel just north of the town. I think we must have fitted in some lunch before going out on the golf course. A few days later Peter drove us to Johannesburg from where we were to fly home on 18 March. On arrival at the airport we were told that our plane would be delayed for several hours. Not wishing to miss a minute, we seized our golf clubs, checked in the rest of our baggage, and shot off and had a round of golf.

In May Bert and Lesley made their first visit to West Hall; they had been to Balgeddie before. In September Bill and Pat Weatherley joined us at Struy.

Earlier that year Angus had qualified as a CA and he and Tina thought they deserved a holiday. They bought a long-wheelbase Land Rover, had it fitted up as a caravanette, and shot off to Guyana on the start of a motor journey round South America. They returned the following March and Angus started working with Barings in the City. He soon decided that the city was not for him and through Barings heard of a job in Sydney. He accepted the job to start in January so, still infected with the travel bug, they drove out to Australia. On arrival they found that the job had melted so they sold their car and returned home. After two years at Cirencester they finally settled in Jersey where they have remained.

Having recorded three family weddings perhaps this would be the appropriate moment to record the fruits thereof:

1970 April, Ian Kirton

1972 January, Clare Kirton

1972 December, Alastair Scoular

1974 January, Lena and Mary Kirton

1974 May, Fiona Spencer-Nairn

1975 April, Michael Spencer-Nairn

1978 April, Anys Scoular

We are now very proud to be the grandparents of eight delightful grandchildren.

# CHAPTER 21

# Retiral

During the first years of the 1970s my responsibilities in Nairn's were reducing and I was looking forward to January 1974 when I would reach retiral age. These last few years had not been the happiest of my forty-three years working with the family firm. However I was now free and could devote more time to the estates of Over Rankeilour and Struy and my other interests such as the church, the hospitals and so on.

I think I should record a little of the history of the property that I inherited on my father's death in 1960, but to do so means going back a few years. Some time before the First World War my grandfather, who owned Rankeilour, bought from the Hopes of Over Rankeilour the home farm and all the land on the south side of the main Cupar–Bow of Fife road. It is a most curious piece of land for the Hopes to have sold, and I suspect my grandfather had his eye on acquiring more of Over Rankeilour, but his death in 1916 put an end to this. Then in 1953, when my father bought Over Rankeilour, he restored the ownership of the home farm to one owner, himself. When he died he left all but two fields of what his father had acquired to me but left the two fields and two strips of woodland with Rankeilour as the pheasants flew better that way. In practice this has left the most ridiculous boundary between the two properties. The total acreage, including West Hall and the Mount Hill, was a little over 1,000, some 600 acres being arable and the rest woodland.

The other property which came my way was Gathercauld and the

foxhound kennels at Harles-
wynd. These were located
about three miles south-east
of Ceres. They had belonged
to Colonel Anstruther-
Thomson of Charlton and it
was he who set up the fox-
hound kennels at Harles-
wynd. When he died the
properties went to his
daughter who had married
Baron Bonde and she and her
husband now spent much of
their time in Sweden.

With Bonny, Colonsay 1983.

When, between the wars,
my father joined Lord Lindsay as joint master, he
thought it would be wise for the kennels to be owned by someone
more directly associated with the foxhounds and he bought them.
The two properties did not adjoin but were separated by a narrow
strip of land belonging to Newbiggin of Craighall, but the water
supply for the kennels came from springs on Gathercauld. About
this time the huntsman Will Hanley retired, having carried the horn
for many years. Father offered Will the small house on Gathercauld
rent free as a retiral home and they remained there until Will died
and Mrs Hanley moved to Leslie House Eventide Home. The Hanleys were great favourites with us. About the time Father died Mr
Melville, who had been the grazing tenant at Gathercauld for many
years, retired and I decided to farm the place. It provided wonderful
summer grazing but proved to be unsuitable for out-wintering cattle, so in 1967 I built a cattle court and silage pit. By this time the
Hanleys had left and I was able to have a stockman on site.

Being a quiet and isolated place it attracted wild life and in March
and April large flocks of geese would graze there. Sometimes there

would be between a thousand and two thousand birds. On one occasion I resolved to try and photograph some of them. I arrived with my zoom lens movie camera and accompanied by Bonny, our Jack Russell terrier, I set off. I approached through a wood and crawled in behind an old dry-stone dyke and there in the field were a mass of birds. I watched them for a few minutes through my binoculars and decided that they were grazing towards me. As I continued to observe them I noticed that they were led by a look-out bird who never lowered her head to feed but kept a very watchful eye in front. As they got nearer she noticed Bonny, who was hunting about at the bottom of the wall. She stopped and watched her for a minute before deciding that she was too small to be any danger to them. After getting some good pictures I showed myself in the hope of getting a picture of them rising from the ground, but this was not too successful.

In 1976 I decided that, in the interests of continuity, it would be beneficial if the foxhounds owned the kennels themselves, so I negotiated a sale which I think has proved beneficial to all parties.

Ever since the war it had been government policy to encourage farmers to increase output and grants were available for new buildings and land drainage. The 1968 gale had made it essential to replace the West Hall cattle courts. After a considerable time researching an ambitious plan for a large cattle feed-lot, the scheme was put into action. It could house about 160 head on slats and included automatic feeding from two large silage towers. When working properly it was most impressive, but Oh! the problem of keeping it going, owing to the corrosive nature of the silage. It lasted about ten years, just about long enough to recover the outlay.

Another large project was a drainage one which was a joint endeavour with my neighbour, Murray Mitchel at Fernie. The survey and technical planning was carried out by the Department of Agriculture and it involved deepening the Fernie burn five feet for a distance of about a mile. This one was a great success and is still proving so.

West Hall.

Of course I was not really a farmer, but what is known by some people a gentleman farmer, one who is almost entirely dependant on the farm manager. I started with Jim Simpson. He had come up through the ranks, was as straight as a die, a bit rugged and rule of thumb but a great pleasure to work with. He was not well during his last few years as he was suffering from cancer and he did not last long after he retired. He was followed by John Sinclair, a college-trained man. John's time was going quite well until his wife went off with the farm foreman and he decided that he could not cope without a housekeeper and left. He was followed by Jim Donald, another college-trained man who came from being assistant manager at Balbirnie. We got on very well with both Jim and his wife and they stayed with us until the place was sold in 1986. Jim still lives in Cupar and has worked for Bell Ingrams of Perth since leaving us.

By 1978 it was becoming clear that our pig operation was not only run down but out of date. The problem was examined in depth with the East of Scotland College of Agriculture special pig advisory unit, and it was determined that if we wished to continue in the production of bacon pigs considerable capital expenditure would be required. Another problem was labour: good pigmen were very difficult to find and weekend relief also difficult. Finally, Jim Donald was not really interested in pigs. I decided to close down the pig unit and invest in a new grain drier and storage unit instead.

For the benefit of those who are not familiar with the district, Over Rankeilour estate is a narrow property stretching from the Mount Hill in the north to where it adjoins Rankeilour in the south. The Mount Hill is quite a prominent feature in the district and is made more so by the presence of a large chimney-like monument which was erected by public subscription in memory of one of the Hopes in recognition of his public service to the community. All the trees on the Mount had been cut down during the war and I replanted all the top area during that wonderful spell when there were no rabbits owing to the ravages of myxomatosis. I carried out a similar replanting programme at Gathercauld where a similar situation existed. This was a wonderful life and there was nothing I enjoyed more than planning drain improvements and woodland improvement schemes.

Although we have made many trips to Jersey to stay with Angus and Tina there are two which stand out in my mind. The first was in July 1977 for Alison Thomas' wedding to Peter Wade. Alison's father David was my first cousin and he and Betty now lived in Sydney, Australia. I had known Alison since she was a little girl living next door to her grandparents Uncle Bruce and Aunt Dorothy at Eurigar. As Peter came from Jersey they decided to have the wedding there and as David and Betty could not get over, Alison asked Angus to give her away. It was quite a small wedding but a very enjoyable one. They now have a boy and a girl.

The second memorable visit was for Christmas 1978. We had

been staying with Mike and Sheila at Otterton so we flew over from
Exeter and were to return there. The outward flight went well but
then the snow came, such snow as never falls in Jersey. The airport
was closed and we could not get out on the appointed day. The next
day they said that they would fly us out to Southampton as Exeter
was closed and take us by bus from there to Exeter. We got to
Southampton all right but by the time we boarded the bus it was
dark. We heard that the roads were very bad with many snow drifts.
We crawled along until about ten o'clock when the driver announced that he was running out of diesel. At the next village he
turned off the main road, jumped out of the bus and disappeared.
After some time he reappeared with a five gallon can. This he
emptied into the bus and went off again to return the empty can.
It was very late when we finally arrived in Exeter airport. We rang
Barton House and Hugh came and picked us up. We have never
tried going to Jersey for Christmas again.

In 1974 I made my final trip to Australia on behalf of the
company. It was a quick one and I flew direct there and back. In
1977 I persuaded Ursula that it would be fun to make a holiday
trip to Australia so we flew at the beginning of February direct to
Perth. We stayed with John and Deb Tomlinson at 103
Labouchere Road, very close to Royal Perth Golf Club. We hired
a car and had a wonderful time visiting all the Devitt relatives and
Harry Hattersley's farm some forty miles south of Perth and of
course played golf. We played one day with Richard and Su
Hattersley and Oh my! was it hot; I think the temperature was
over 100°F. At the end of February we flew to Melbourne and
hired another car. We drove out to Mortlake to stay with Bill
and Pat Weatherley; here we met his brother and his wife, also his
two sons James and Richard and their families. What a joy it was
to have no business dates to keep!

On returning to Melbourne we played another game of golf in a
temperature over 100°F, but the thing we remember most about
that round was the flies. While there we dined with Michael and

Dargie Nairn and we also met Hugh Gillies, Tina's brother who was working out there at the time. From Melbourne we drove up through the Snowy Mountains and on to Canberra and finally down to Sydney: here we were based once more in Bert and Mary's flat. There followed a great social round of visits, dinner parties, cocktail parties and of course golf at both Royal Sydney and Elenora.

After all this festivity we drove north, visiting Tom and Rosalind Cropper at Willow Tree, Heather and Angus Kirton at Caringa and on to Old Banalbo to see Jocelyn. On the return journey we called on Dr Thomas, Uncle Bruce's nephew who lived near Newcastle. We had met them when he had been working in Victoria Hospital in Kirkcaldy. We flew direct home from Sydney at the end of March.

Some years before this, probably about the late 1960s, Ursula and I joined Peter and June Devitt to stay with Mr and Mrs Tony Woodcock in Kampala, Uganda. Tony was the manager of Barclay's Bank in Kampala and he and his wife were kindness itself. We played golf one day on a course where the fairways were lined with the bush. The only problem was getting to your ball before a small dark figure disappeared with it into the bush.

Tony sent us off in his large Ford Granada with a driver to the Princess Elizabeth game park; the trip was to cover three days. Uganda, although it lies astride the equator, is high and has a reasonable rainfall. I was most impressed with the country which was hilly and very green and at that time was prosperous with a good export trade in coffee, bananas and other things. All the people looked well clothed, including the children. This was in the early days of Obote and before General Amin seized power.

After quite a long drive we arrived at the game park camp. Next morning we were taken out in quite a small boat by two wardens. There seemed to be hippos everywhere and the wardens passed so close to them they could poke them with their paddles. There were masses of the most colourful birds and we were able to pass very close to what looked to me to be a very old bull elephant. In the afternoon our wardens took us in a Land Rover where once again we passed through herds of buffalo and one of female elephants most of which had small calves. The next morning we spent looking for some tree-climbing lions which we were informed were peculiar to this district. We found one lying most comfortably in the fork of a tree about twelve feet from the ground. We got fairly close and I got some quite good photographs. In the afternoon we returned to Kampala. What a lovely holiday that was.

Some years later, now all OAPs, Howson and Elizabeth Devitt, Ursula and I booked a fourteen-day safari holiday in Kenya and Tanzania. We flew to Nairobi where we arrived about lunch time, and booked into our hotel where we were to spend one night. After a free afternoon we attended a briefing meeting at which we were told that there would be six persons to a mini-bus and that there would be a driver and guide with each. The guide would know where to go and be responsible to ensure our accommodation and comfort at all times. 'Please do not leave the bus without the permission of the guide.' We were able to arrange that there would only be the four of us in our bus. We were introduced to our guide who said he would meet us in the hall with our baggage next morning. The mini-bus had a sliding roof which permitted us to stand up to take photographs.

After crossing the border into Tanzania we entered the Serengeti Plain. The country was flat and covered with scrub and small trees interspersed with open spaces. Our guide took us down tracks off the main road. I can't remember what this bunch of wide eyed tourists first saw but before long there was a huge rhino. As we approached it our bus took a lurch to one side and the driver announced that we had a puncture. We were some 25 yards from our rhino which did not appear to have noticed us and stood chewing the cud. The driver and guide changed the wheel while we kept it under observation. After some time it just wandered off as if it had never seen us.

On arrival at a camp our guide checked our accommodation, took our bags into our rooms and arranged to meet us in the lounge before dinner. He dined with us each night and about 10 p.m. we went to our rooms. From time to time we met other vehicles and we usually stopped and exchanged news.

On one such an occasion we learnt that there was supposed to be a leopard up a tree quite near. We found the tree and our driver attempted to drive round it, but when right under the branches our front wheels stuck in a small ditch and we could go neither back or forward. Fortunately a Land Rover appeared and the white driver drove up behind us, produced a rope and pulled us out. Full of gratitude we asked him to stop and have a drink with us. We joined him in the shade of an acacia tree. Out of the Land Rover a girl, dressed only in a bikini, emerged. These two were on their own and we all agreed that it was time for lunch. While we were chewing away someone said, 'Look!' and there was a cheetah walking towards us. It stopped, gave us a casual glance, walked a few more paces and slumped down under a tree.

After a day or two, during which we saw all sorts of game, we arrived at the Ngorongoro Crater. This is several miles in diameter and has quite steep sides. Our two nights and a day were quite fascinating. In the morning we were driven down a steep track onto the floor of the crater and spent the day driving around inside. The amount of game there was quite staggering. We saw pink flamingos and masses of wildebeest which were just at the calving with lots of little calves. There were zebra, impala, hyenas, hippos, lions, elephants, jackals and I am sure a lot more. The impala grazed quite close to the sleeping lions and paid little attention to them so long as they did not get up.

Next day we returned to Nairobi. We were sorry to say good-bye to our driver and guide, both of whom had been not only efficient but good company.

The following day we flew down to Mombassa. There was no fixed programme for our stay here; you were free to do what you liked. We heard that there was another reserve not too far away so we hired a car, bought a map and planned to set off early next morning. We found Lake Manyara National Park without difficulty and what a beautiful place it was, being situated along the shores of the lake. We had no guide but with our map we found our way quite easily. Elephants and giraffe were very numerous, but I don't remember seeing any carnivores. One thing which delighted us was to find a small herd of sable antelope, which we were told were getting very scarce. After a glorious day in beautiful surroundings we returned to our hotel.

During this trip Howson and I agreed that he would take still photographs and I would take movies and that we would swap copies on our return. Our holiday was now nearing its end and we flew back to Nairobi and on to London.

We are back now at Struy. Ever since the war I had become more and more interested in the Rough Wood, the old Caledonian Forest section of Struy, and its preservation. I raised this problem with the Nature Conservancy who were most sympathetic but said they had no money to help. By the early 1970s conservation was becoming more popular and funds were becoming more available, so I raised the matter again. This time they suggested that if I was prepared to have the area made a nature reserve they could help, but it would be better if Culligran and Braulin were included. My nephew Frank, at Culligran, readily agreed but Lord Lovat, who owned Braulin, refused. A formal agreement was signed in 1977 and has worked very well since.

By this time Angus was the owner of Struy as I had given it to him as a wedding present. Ursula and I remained the tenants. As the years passed the cost of running and maintaining the lodge was becoming quite a burden and looked like getting worse. We held a family conference at which we decided that the only thing to do was to replace the present lodge with a modern one. I asked an architect in Inverness for ideas, but those he produced were quite hopeless – he obviously had not listened to us – so we dropped him.

I then started testing the kit home market and found Guildway, who were prepared to co-operate and try to meet our requirements. They said that if I would produce drawings using their standard modules they would check them and if approved they would produce the working drawings. I went to work and produced about a dozen possibilities before Ursula, Tina and Angus finally approved one. What fun I had; this was something I really enjoyed.

We realised that we would require a builder to do the demolition, the site work foundations and provide the other services. It just so happened that Guildway's Scottish agent lived in Nairn so I asked his advice. He recommended Tulloch's of Nairn and brought along Mr Sandy Tulloch. He was a splendid man and a great help in obtaining planning permission. By February 1980 Guildway's drawings were about ready so I said to Sandy, 'We want to be in by mid September. What is your deadline for getting the word to go to meet that date?' He replied that if we said go by 1 April we would be in by mid September. This was done and we moved in on 12 September. I think this must be a world record: the old house demolished and the replacement built in just over four months.

We stored all the furniture in the farmhouse, the one that Sarah and John have now. It was so crowded that there was only a little space round the stove and enough for two mattresses on the floor of one of the bedrooms. While the building was on we were up at Struy every week and camped in this house. Such are modern facilities that we can arrive at the new lodge any time of year and be comfortable, with hot water and heating in ninety minutes. With eleven beds we can continue to have all our friends to stay with half the effort and twice the convenience.

It was at this same time that we dispersed the cattle. Winter feeding was proving too expensive, and the making of silage too difficult. As the result of this decision George Manson became redundant. We offered him free tenancy of his house and a small honorarium in return for him looking after all the house property and the cutting of the grass round the lodge. George got another job, first with the quarry and later with the roads department. How lucky we have been with our two employees, George and Henry, and with all those who went before them.

Back in 1966 when we decided to live in West Hall and not Over Rankeilour I began looking for a tenant, then suddenly, my cousin Donald Black said, 'I have a tenant for you, Neil Stewart-Meiklejohn.' Donald and Neil had served together in the Black Watch. Neil had just sold his large house and property in Perthshire and was looking for somewhere to house himself and his furniture. They moved in in early 1967. They gave up their lease in 1981 and so once more the house was empty. I wondered if it would make a good country club and golf course but the Department of Agriculture refused to release the land for that purpose; as it turned out this was probably just as well. Angus and I, after some soul searching, decided that we would offer it for sale, and it was sold in 1984 to Mr David Glass. I was now seventy-five and began thinking that it was about time I gave up farming and so began discussing the whole future of Over Rankeilour with Angus.

Some time towards the end of 1985 Ursula had a problem and Dr McDonald diagnosed gall bladder trouble and referred her to a Mr McIntyre in Edinburgh. He recommended the removal of the gall bladder and so she went into the Murrayfield Hospital early in January and had it out. You should have seen her hospital room – it was more like a florist's shop. She got on well but it takes time to get over that operation.

In January 1986 we decided to put the whole place on the market and called in Colin Strang-Steel of Frank Knight and Rutley. He advised us that it would probably be the autumn before it could be sold. This suited us as it gave us time to look for somewhere to live. Within less than two weeks the agents were on the telephone asking if they could bring a young couple to view the place. We said, 'Yes, of course,' and an early date was fixed.

On the appointed day a delightful young couple called Crombie arrived. Almost immediately Evelyn said to Ursula, 'I was at school with a Spencer-Nairn'; of course this was Catriona and this led on to the discovery that Ursula had been at school with her mother. After the inspection the Crombies asked if they could have the place in May. We agreed that they could have the farm in May but not the house as we had nowhere to go. It was agreed that we could have until October to evacuate the house.

Almost the next day Sarah arrived to see how her mother was after her operation. Sarah went into Cupar to do some shopping and, walking down the street, noticed in a lawyer's window that Baltilly was for sale. Now, Sarah knew Baltilly as, many years before, she had been to parties with the Prains who lived there at that time. She rushed home and said, 'I have found you a house, Baltilly!' We rang the agents and went to see it that afternoon. Within days we had had the survey done and made an offer which was accepted with occupancy in May. So there we were with the farm sold and us with a new home, all within the space of three weeks.

In April Angus suggested that it would do his mother good if we joined them for a week's holiday in Spain. They were taking their children down there for tennis coaching. This was to be a rest cure for us so we hired a car and pottered about, including a visit to Gibraltar. On the day of our departure we handed over our car at the airport and strolled over to the airport building. On the way I suddenly felt a sharp pain in my left achilles tendon. It remained painful all the way home where I went to the doctor to be told that I had damaged the tendon. I received injections of cortisone but this did no good so I was stuck in plaster.

As soon as we knew that Baltilly was to be ours we knew that we could not live in it as it was with its basement kitchen, so out came the pencil and drawing board and before long we had found the solution. Time was not on our side and we had two hurdles to overcome in obtaining planning permission. The house was a B listed building which meant we had to have our plans passed not only by the local planning authority but also by

St Andrews House, Edinburgh. We engaged a Cupar architect who drew the plans to our sketch drawings and what joy when they passed both authorities. Our plan included adding a kitchen with garage under it on the east side of the house and this of course had to be in stone to match the existing house. Once again we were in luck as Kilmaron had been demolished and we obtained stone from there.

We knew from the start that it was going to be a race against time as not only was there the extension but the house had to be rewired and many other alterations made. As there was to be little or no alteration in the basement our plan was to get one bedroom habitable and the two basement rooms and then move in while the rest of the work was going on. Everything therefore was concentrated on getting the existing building finished before starting the extension. By September we were approaching this position and I had now been out of plaster for some weeks, and we were planning to go down to Catriona's wedding to George Tremlett on 5 September.

Then suddenly I had a new problem. We were at Baltilly, about the 3rd, and I trod on a small piece of wood. What pain shot up my leg; my tendon had really broken this time. The pain went quite quickly but I could not move my foot up or down. A quick telephone call revealed that Mr Lamb, the surgeon I had been attending, was in Hong Kong and would not be back till the next week. As we were due to fly down next day we decided to leave the leg until we returned when Mr Lamb would be home. The leg did not hurt much but it made me very lame.

The weekend including the wedding went very well and on our return Ursula drove me to Murrayfield Hospital to see Mr Lamb. He took one look at it and said, 'You come in here tomorrow; I shall have to operate on it.'

Home we went and back next day. I cannot remember which day the operation was but when I came to I was back in plaster.

October was almost on us and we had to be out of West Hall by the end of the month. Every effort was directed to make enough room in the house and coach house to accommodate all our belongings, including furniture. Finally, on 23 October, we moved, and I am glad to say I was out of plaster again. This was our fourth home in fifty-one years, and I hope the last.

I think I should record that on 25 October 1985 we celebrated our Golden Wedding with a small family party at Struy; the party was shared with Frank and Juliet whose tenth anniversary it was. This was followed by a large cocktail party in Fernie Castle Hotel in Fife.

The move to Baltilly was a great change for me. I had never lived anywhere except on an estate, except for the two brief years at Lahill. There was always so much to do on an estate: cleaning ditches, pruning trees, cutting nettles, all things I loved to do. It was a wonderful life, especially after I retired. However Baltilly had a beautiful walled garden and fifteen acres in all so there was enough to start me off.

On Tuesday 28 July 1987 I was working in the garden opposite the front door when I saw a car draw up. I went over to see who it was and found Catherine Russel who informed me that Ursula had fallen in Cupar and broken her leg and that she had been taken to the Dundee Royal Infirmary. I rang the hospital to be told that she had not been seen by the doctor and that I should ring back later. This I did, to get the same answer, so I got in the car and went over. I had to be back at Leuchars station at seven to meet Ursula's cousin Monica who was already on the train.

When I arrived at the hospital I found Ursula who had just come out of X-ray and the report was a broken femur. I was told that she would be operated on the following morning. She told me that she had been crossing the narrow bit of the Bonnygate and had tripped on the pavement and fallen. She was certain she had broken her leg so insisted that she be not moved and an ambulance called. Amongst others who came to the rescue was Catherine's daughter

who told her mother that Ruth Hutchison Bradburne had broken
her leg. Ruth had been dead about four years. I left saying I would
bring Monica over the next afternoon, by which time the operation
would be over. I picked up Monica at seven and returned to Baltilly.

The next afternoon we found Ursula in a geriatric ward. All had
gone well and she was quite cheerful. We visited her again on
Thursday and Friday and each time found her a little more upset
by the other patients. At 6.00 a.m. on Saturday morning she was on
the telephone saying, 'I can't stand it here, you must get me out,
ring up Mr Dent.' She then put down the telephone. Mr Dent was
the surgeon who had done the operation. I was doubtful if he would
be on duty on Saturday, but when I rang he was there. I explained
what had happened and he said he would go and see Ursula and
ring me back.

When he arrived she pleaded with him to let her out. He
explained that it was most unusual to be let home so soon but after
a trial run with a zimmer he said she could go but must be back
for a check on Monday morning. When Monica and I arrived she
was brought to the car in a wheeled chair, but with a zimmer. At
Baltilly, with the aid of the zimmer, a garden chair on wheels and
the lift we got her up to bed. By Monday morning she was managing the zimmer quite well so we dispensed with the garden chair.
The trip to Dundee was uneventful and from then on she slowly
became more mobile.

We went up to Struy as usual and it was nice to be on the hill
again, having missed the last season through flitting and broken
tendons. My problem this season was my right eye which finally
packed up and I had to spy and shoot off my left shoulder.

We returned to Baltilly on 21 October and I parked the Subaru
and trailer at the front door. I was unloading a large but light box
from the back of the car when I caught my right toe in the trailer
safety wire and crashed to the ground. Like Ursula I knew I had
broken a bone. Ursula dialled 999 and a strange doctor and
ambulance appeared. It was the same driver who had taken Ursula

to hospital so off we went to the Dundee Royal Infirmary. Ursula rang Mr Turner, the senior consultant, and warned me in. The X-ray showed that I had done almost the same thing as Ursula. I landed up in the male casualty ward and had my pin and plate fitted next morning. That went very well but I developed bladder trouble and could not spend a penny. The ward doctor told me to drink more which proved to be quite the wrong thing.

It was obvious that I was not going to get out as quickly as Ursula and she organised for me to be moved to Fernbrae Nursing Home. In the meantime I was in considerable pain and asked to see a senior doctor. Mr Turner said he would arrange for Mr Baxby, the urologist, to see me. Before he came I was taken off to Fernbrae, and Mr Baxby caught up with me that evening. He was alarmed at the tightness of my bladder and popped in a catheter. Oh! what a relief; I deflated like a balloon. My problem proved to be prostate and I was given the option of having it dealt with now or waiting till my leg was better. I opted to have it done immediately although it would slow my getting back on my feet. The operation was done but another minor problem emerged which required a second minor operation, all of which meant that my total stay in hospital was a month.

Strangely enough my sister Clare was also in Fernbrae, having had a kidney removed by Mr Baxby. Neither of us was mobile so we could not visit one another. We discovered that Keith Baxby was a keen stalking man and he has now been to Struy several times. 1992 was to prove to be my last stalking season, but although my eyesight was deteriorating I managed to shoot one stag seventy-one years after shooting my first one. Sadly, in November, my eyes suddenly got a lot worse and I gave up driving; and it was not long before Dr Coliero certified me as partially sighted.

During the 1980s we stayed in Combe House Hotel, Gittisham, East Devon, to attend various Devitt family celebrations including Mike and Sheila's Golden Wedding, Peter's eightieth birthday and Howson and Elizabeth's Golden Wedding. When in 1992 the twins,

The gathering for my 80th birthday lunch. *Back row, left to right:* Tina (daughter in law), Frank (brother), Clare (sister), Angus (son), George Tremlett (son-in-law), Catriona Tremlett (daughter), John Scoular (son-in-law), Sarah Scoular (daughter). *Front:* Alastair, Ursula.

Ursula and Sheila, were to reach their eightieth on 19 December they decided to celebrate it at Combe and that all available children and grandchildren be invited to stay. On the day we sat down twenty-six for dinner, twenty-two of whom were staying in the hotel. Mike and I arranged that we would all assemble before dinner and have drinks served and that the twins would then make a triumphal entry, followed by the cutting of the cake; and that Richard would propose his aunts' healths. This set the party off to a very good start and many photographs were taken. John Boswell, who with his wife ran the hotel and whom we now knew quite well, suggested that he laid on a family breakfast for all those staying in the hotel which we thought was a splendid idea. After a very good dinner, the revelry amongst the young continued to quite a late hour. Breakfast was to be at nine and Ursula thought that some of the young were bound to be late so did not hurry down. Eventually one of our grandchildren came up and told us that the whole company was sitting waiting her arrival. What a breakfast we had; there was a serving table loaded with every form of breakfast food from which we helped ourselves. It made a very fitting end to a very good weekend.

On 1 March 1993 Ursula, Helen Nairn and I flew out to Madeira for a two-week holiday. We stayed at the Savoy Hotel which we found very good. We took life very quietly and we tried the swimming pool but found it too cold. We took two long drives. I had no idea the island was so mountainous and steep, nor that bananas were an even more important export than wine.

Baltilly Ho., 1988.

Claudia and Ben Carnegie arrived in the hotel for the second week, which was nice. We very, very much enjoyed having Helen with us.

In the beginning of June we flew south and were met by Catriona, with whom we stayed. She took us to my sister Matilda's eightieth birthday party which was held at her youngest son Michael's house. Catriona then ran us down and left us with Mike and Sheila. After a day or two there Mike put us on a plane at Exeter for Guernsey where we had lunch with my brother Frank before flying on to stay in Jersey with Angus and Tina. From there we flew direct back to Edinburgh.

That was the last time we saw Mike. He had had a hip operation earlier in the year which relieved him of much pain, but very soon after our visit he got a terrible pain and was taken into hospital. I think there was a clot somewhere and he died at the end of July. We flew down for the funeral and once again stayed with Catriona. George drove us all the way down to Otterton and we only just got there in time. After lunch at Barn House we motored up to Hawkerage for the interment. From there George drove us back to their home. It was a long day but fortunately the weather was beautiful. The next day we flew home again. This was a very sad day for us. Mike, Howson and I had all been at Trinity Hall together, and Mike and I had married Howson's twin sisters so we had been life-long friends as well as being brothers-in-law. Sheila continues to live alone at Barn House and I am afraid finds it very lonely.

In the spring of 1994 we flew down to Catriona's for Ian's confirmation. While there Catriona took us to see several semi-local friends and in addition drove us all the way to Devon to see Sheila. She was in the local cottage hospital for a few days with some minor problem but otherwise she seemed well. Poor Sheila's memory is failing but she manages in her own home with some outside assistance.

In the autumn we were back at Struy enjoying one of the warmest seasons I can remember and with a string of wonderful guests coming and going, when on 3 October a slight calamity occurred. It was about 7.45, and Ursula and I had just changed for dinner and set off for the drawing room when we bumped into young John Gilmour who was late off the hill. I expected her to say something to him but she paused for a minute, then brushed past him and went to get a bottle for dinner. I continued on my way. Almost immediately, Jane, who was cooking for us, said, 'You had better come; there is something wrong with Mrs Nairn.' By the time I got there Clare and several other ladies were there who told me that Ursula was unable to speak. Some of them took Ursula off to bed and Clare and I went and rang the doctor. It was about forty-five minutes before he arrived, by which time she was speaking but not normally. He diagnosed a small stroke and said she was lucky as nothing else was affected and that it was almost certain that she should recover altogether. She was ordered to go slow for some weeks. Ursula explained to me later that when she met John not a word would come out, so partly in panic she pushed past him and then when she met Jane she could not speak to her either. If it had to happen, that was the moment, as we had seven wonderful guests and a resident cook who quickly had everything under control. It meant that she could not play golf and somewhat spoilt the rest of her time at Struy. In the meantime I finished the season with three salmon, thanks to some super amateur gillies.

We are now looking forward to 25 October 1995 when we will celebrate our Diamond Wedding.

# CHAPTER 22

# My faith and where it led me

The foundations of my Christian faith, as I have already mentioned, were laid by my mother at a very early age. Almost as soon as we could speak we were taught to say our prayers at our mother's knee. 'God bless Daddy and Mummy and make me a good boy, Amen.' As we grew, so the content of our prayer increased. The next step was Mother reading bible stories to us after lunch on Sundays. All this time we were being taught the do's and don'ts of our faith. We were encouraged to do the do's and helped to resist doing the don'ts. By this means we developed a capability to react automatically in the right way. Of course we transgressed often but I am sure this training made life easier later. My parents went to church on Sunday so that must be the proper thing to do; in fact we looked forward to the day when we would be allowed to go.

The Bow Kirk was a large rectangular building with a gallery across the back. My parents sat in the front row of the gallery, while my grandparents and various aunts sat in the two back pews on the left side downstairs. The first time I went to church we sat in the front row of the gallery and were sent out with a nursemaid before the sermon and so we grew up just knowing that there was a God, a God who loved us and could do all sorts of wonderful things, but also one who always knew when you did wrong. We did not of course think about these things much; we just accepted it.

When I went to Cargilfield I am afraid nightly prayers lapsed but

we went to church at Cramond on Sunday, and of course we went
to church in the holidays.

When I went to Shrewsbury, church changed. I had been brought
up in a Scottish Free Kirk and now had to get used to the Anglican
form of service and there were such new things as choir boys in
surplices. We attended a short service in chapel every day and went
twice on Sunday. I enjoyed chapel, the singing was good and I
experienced some inexplicable uplift from it.

I was not confirmed at school but joined the Bow Kirk, under
the Rev. William McCraw, on leaving school.

At Cambridge I am afraid I did not attend Chapel, making the
excuse to myself that it was Anglican and I was now a Presbyterian.
I made no attempt to find a Presbyterian church. Now, having a
private bedroom, I restarted bedside prayers. The content of those
prayers was much more selfish than it should have been, but still,
it was a start.

By the time I had left Cambridge I had met Ursula and there was
no doubt that there was some sort of relationship between us. This
can't be for real, I thought, I have met so few girls it's probably just
a flash in the pan.

As the years passed this attraction grew ever stronger and other
girls did not interest me. I prayed so hard for guidance and finally
this canny Scot made up his mind in 1935.

Wasn't I lucky that I hadn't lost her? I knew that Ursula was a
believer, having grown up as I had done in a Christian home, and
we were able to share our faith. Of course, over the last fifty-nine
years we have had our arguments but we have always been able to
resolve them on our knees at our bedside. The other occasion when
I desperately needed help was when Ian was killed. In answer to
my prayers I received the clearest message. 'Ian is now safe with
me; this is no time for self pity. I still have work for you to do and
I will be with you.'

When we moved to Balgeddie we became members of Christ's
Kirk on the Green, Leslie. I knew the minister, the Rev.

Drummond-Page, as we had attended regularly there since moving to Leslie in 1920. I cannot recall any specific incident during the war that had any special influence on me, but I was very grateful that I had come through without even a scratch, and, perhaps even more importantly, no memories of any horrific happenings.

After the war Mr Page invited me to join the Kirk Session and I was ordained an elder in October 1946. Shortly afterwards it was announced that the Rev. D. P. Thomson, the Evangelist for the Church of Scotland, would be leading a campaign in Kirkcaldy and that he would welcome volunteer workers from any congregation in the Presbytery. Ursula and I volunteered. The general plan was that every home in the town would be visited by a pair of volunteers during the week of the campaign. We met for an evening meal together at which we received our instructions and were paired off. Husbands and wives did not work together. We visited every home, regardless of who lived there, and I don't remember not being welcomed. One had some quite interesting experiences. I remember diving up a pend then up an outside stair to a door which appeared to lead only to an attic. Inside there was one fair sized room with an open fire. There were two box beds on either side and a bare table in the middle. The occupants were two young women and several small children We had a very happy chat during which we discovered that both their husbands were in prison. I don't know how much good we did but we learnt a lot.

About this time I was approached by an industrial chaplain, who invited me to join a group of people from industry to study what further missionary work could usefully be done there. We held meetings in Glasgow on Saturday afternoons and local ones for foremen, workers and managers. The group was called Scottish Christian Industrial Order (SCIO). It kept going for some years but eventually petered out.

When in the early 1950s Father was negotiating with the Church of Scotland about the hand-over of Leslie House I got to know

Rev. Dr Cameron who was convener of the committee of Social Responsibility. The result was I found myself Chairman of the local Leslie House Committee. It was not long before I found myself on the General Finance Committee of the Church of Scotland and a special committee called the Committee anent Administration which had been set up to see what changes should be made in the committee system of the Church. I also became a commissioner to the General Assembly one year.

In 1972 I started a four-year stint as convener of the Finance Committee and, as such, an ex-officio member of fourteen other committees. As convener I had to make the report to the General Assembly on the financial position of the church. I can remember standing up in front of that packed hall and trying to read my speech. That was bad enough but when the questions came it was worse. I am afraid I am no public speaker and did not do the subject justice. However, it had to be done for another three years. I much enjoyed this work and gained a very wide knowledge of the workings of the Church of Scotland.

Having handed over my convenership, I was asked to serve on what was called the Committee of 40. The task of this committee was to review again the management structure of the church and make recommendations. We met sometimes in 121 George Street but sometimes we had two-day meetings in Dunblane. One of the main recommendations in our report was the setting up of the Assembly Council and I became one of the founder members.

About 1969 I took over the treasurership of Monimail Parish Church from Iain Fraser and kept the job for twenty years. During that period we had a linkage with Springfield, the breaking of that link and the formation of the link with Creich, Flisk and Kilmany Parish. We also had the sale of the kirk and manse at the Bow. All this involved quite a lot of complicated financial negotiations; I think my years in 121 were a help. I served as an elder on St Andrew's Presbytery from about 1969 to 1989. I hope and pray that

I may have been able to contribute something towards the furtherance of God's Kingdom here on Earth.

To those who have stayed with me this far I now say Good-bye and God Bless You.

# Nairns of Kirkcaldy

It was a sad day for many of us when Nairn Williamson were taken over by Lever Bros. Why was it necessary?

I have now been retired for over twenty years and although I was involved almost to the end I think I, after all these years, can make a fair assessment of what happened. To do so I must go quite a long way back in history.

Before the First World War the industry grew, keeping pace with the growth in the UK economy and that of the Dominions, who were very good customers. In spite of the growth competition was keen, particularly between Michael Nairn and James Williamson of Lancaster. Lord Ashton, who owned Williamson's, determined not to be beaten by Nairn and was very suspicious of any Nairn even entering Lancaster. My father told me that he visited Lancaster on one occasion and was immediately approached by Lord Ashton asking what he was doing there.

After the first war the manufacturers got together and formed the Linoleum Manufacturers' Association. The object of this body was to standardise gauges (thicknesses) and prices. This meant that competition was forced into bigger ranges and patterns, all of which forced up stock levels and led to other uneconomic practices.

There followed the Second World War during which most companies were very much involved in war work. After the war there was a huge change in the world economy and many new products appeared to compete with linoleum, such as vinyls and tufted carpets. This new competition forced several of the smaller companies out of business and finally led to the merger of Nairn's and Williamson's.

In the late 1800s the company was run by my grandfather, the first Sir Michael Nairn; and he was assisted by his brother John and a very good team they made. About 1890 Sir Michael's eldest daughter married William Black and he joined the company. He never had a very senior position but he did have a large family including two sons: Willie, born about 1898 and Michael, born a year or two later.

Sir Michael's elder son Michael had started in the company by this time and he was followed by my father Robert Spencer-Nairn, known as Spencer in 1901.

My father had joined the Territorial Army, so in 1914 he was called up for war service and did not return until after the war. On reaching military age, first Willie and then Michael joined up and both saw service in France.

In 1916 Sir Michael died in his car while being driven from his home, Rankeilour, to Kirkcaldy. He was succeeded as Chairman by his brother John. John's only son Ian was killed in France in the last year of the war. Soon after the war ended, John died and was succeeded by the new Sir Michael. By this time Willie and Michael had been demobilised and so of course had my father. Both the Black boys were found places in the company, Willie on the sales side with father, and Michael in the factory under Sir Michael. In 1928 my brother Douglas joined, I followed in 1930 followed by George, Sir Michael's son, and finally my young brother Frank in 1932. There were now six cousins with the hereditary heir the youngest of them all. In 1939 five of the six left as TA members, but the government decided that one must be withdrawn to help with the war work and this fell on Frank.

When the war ended, believe it or not, we all returned but unfortunately George had lost his left eye at Dunkirk. By this time Uncle Mike was seventy-one and Father was sixty-five. Almost immediately Douglas left the company owing to matrimonial problems and Frank, who was a junior member of the family, decided to seek a place with Congoleum Nairn where his prospects might be better. This left four cousins, none of whom had the training or experience to fit them for the very new and challenging times which lay ahead. Willie Black was the right age but I don't think he was favoured by Uncle Mike or my father and Michael was unfit, having been gassed in the war, and in fact he died in 1947.

We muddled on for a time with, in the late 1950s, the load finally falling on George's shoulders with me as joint Managing Director. We proved to be a weak and indecisive team who made many mistakes, thus the firm finished up as it did. If only Uncle Mike and Father had had the foresight to see that a bunch of cousins could not form a strong management team and either pulled one out for special training or brought someone in, things might have been different.